Advanced Combat Ju-jutsu
- Entrance to Secrets

Published by:

Modern Bu-jutsu Inc
P.O. Box 703-A
Westmont, IL 60559

Warning

The material included in this book is for educational purposes and to promote continued self-defense training.

The self-defense method in the book are not guaranteed by the author to work or to be safe at any time.

In some situations, applications of the techniques may not be warranted or allowable under local, state, or federal laws. No representations are made by the author or Modern Bu-jutsu regarding the appropriateness or legality of their use.

The techniques should be practiced under a licensed Miyama Ryu instructor. Before trying any of these techniques, which could cause injury, you should consult a doctor. The author and Modern Bu-jutsu are not responsible if any such injury occurs.

Secrets of Advanced Combat Ju-jutsu, 2nd edition
Originally published as Advanced Combat Ju-jutsu - Entrance to Secrets
Copyright © 1992, 1993 D'Arcy J. Rahming

All rights reserved. No part of this publication may be reproduced, stored in a retrieval system, or transmitted, in any form or by any means, electronic, mechanical, photocopying, recording or otherwise, without the prior written permission of the author.
Library of Congress#: 92-61754
ISBN: 0-9627898-8-7

Acknowledgments:

Technical consultant: Shinan Pereira, 6th dan Judo, San Moku Roku Sosuishin Ryu Ju-jutsu
Editor: Jennifer Harris Baarman
Summary Editor: Benita Rahming
Technical Editor: Demetrios Milliaressis, Kaiden Miyama Ryu
Technical Editor: Eileen Adams de Pereira, Kaiden Miyama Ryu
Illustrations and cover: Steven Taylor
Photos: Ralph Mazzaro
Uke: Arthur Steinberger

Dedication:

To the future generations of Miyama Ryu students.

Table of Contents

Foreword	Pg 9
About the Author	Pg 10
Introduction	Pg 11
Potrait of Shinan	Pg 12
Classical Ju-jutsu	Pg 13
History	Pg 14
Interview	Pg 15, 16
Zanshin:	Pg 17
Fudoshin:	Pg 18
Kihon	Pg 19, 20

Taiso — Pg 21

Ukemi
Side/rear	Pg 22
Front roll/free	Pg 23
Front fall/twisting	Pg 24
Kote-gaeshi/Aiki	Pg 25
Somersault	Pg 26

Atemi Waza
Hand strikes	Pg 28
More hand strikes	Pg 29
Kicks	Pg 30

Kote Waza
Kote-gaeshi 1	Pg 31
Kote-gaeshi 2	Pg 32
Kote-gaeshi 3	Pg 33
Kote-gaeshi 4	Pg 34
Kote-gaeshi 5	Pg 35
Kote-gaeshi 6	Pg 36
Kote-gaeshi 7	Pg 37
Kote-gaeshi 8	Pg 38
Compound Kote-gaeshi	Pg 39
Shiho-nage	Pg 40
Pendulum	Pg 41
Nikyo basic/forearm	Pg 42
Sankyo	Pg 43
Controls	Pg 44

Kansetsu Waza
Waki-gatame	Pg 45
Waki-gatame wrist	Pg 46
Ude-garami	Pg 47
Hammerlock	Pg 48
Devil's handshake	Pg 49
Armbars	Pg 50
Tigerlock/control	Pg 51

Nage Waza
Ippon Seoi nage	Pg 52
Koshi-guruma	Pg 53
Uki otoshi	Pg 54
Osoto-gari	Pg 55
Sukuinage	Pg 56
Kosoto-gari	Pg 57
Ogoshi	Pg 58
Uki-goshi	Pg 59
Ju-jutsu Tai-otoshi	Pg 60
Harai-goshi	Pg 61
Judo Tai-otoshi	Pg 62
Yama-arashi (2 ways)	Pg 63
Ouchi-gari	Pg 64
Kouchi-gari	Pg 65
Morote Seoi nage	Pg 66
Tomoe nage	Pg 67
Uki waza	Pg 68
Osoto-guruma	Pg 69
Kata-guruma	Pg 70
Sode tsuri komi-goshi	Pg 71
Soto makikomi (3 ways)	Pg 72
Tsuri-goshi	Pg 73
Hane-goshi	Pg 74
Hane makikomi	Pg 75
Uchi mata	Pg 76
Hiza-guruma	Pg 77
Sasae tsurikomi ashi	Pg 78
Ushiro-goshi	Pg 79
Hasamae-gaeshi (front)	Pg 80
Hasamae-gaeshi (rear)	Pg 81
Ushiro-guruma	Pg 82

Table of Contents

Osae-komi Waza
Uke on back — Pg 83
Uke on stomach — Pg 84
Uke on stomach/side — Pg 85

Tai sabaki
Basic — Pg 88 - 94
Uraken — Pg 95 - 99
Catsteps — Pg 100 - 104
Kicking — Pg 105 - 109
With throws — Pg 110 - 119

The Warrior's Strategy — Pg 120, 121

Wrist grabs — Pg 122 - 125

Lapel grabs — Pg 126 - 130

Rear body grabs — Pg 131,132

Front body grabs — Pg 133-136

Mugs 1-17 — Pg 137-153

Chokes — Pg 154 - 156

Knife defenses — Pg 157 - 168

Club defenses — Pg 169 - 174

Gun defenses — Pg 175 - 179

Multiple man attacks — Pg 180

Aiding someone — Pg 182

Kick defenses — Pg 183 - 185

Sitting defenses — Pg 186 - 189

Ground defenses — Pg 190 - 192

Wall techniques — Pg 195,196

Reversals — Pg 197 - 203

Kyu Exams — Pg 205 - 213

Miyama Ryu Gokyo — Pg 215

Black Belt Exams — Pg 216-219

Black Belt Register — Pg 220 - 226

Index — Pg 227

Foreword

As Co-Chairman of the Miyama Ryu Ju-jutsu Executive Board, it is an honor for me to forward Mr. Rahming's book **Advanced Combat Ju-jutsu- Entrance to Secrets**. Mr. Rahming is a dedicated martial artist and instructor whose previous works have greatly contributed to the resurgence in the study of Ju-jutsu.

Miyama Ryu continues to develop as a modern martial art whose techniques, while based on the principles of classical Ju-jutsu, have been adapted to situations prevalent within our modern society. When Shinan Pereira first started teaching Ju-jutsu the title "Keeper of the Lost Art" was fondly used by many. It is coincidental that this work comes at a time when we at the Hombo Dojo are witnessing the renewed vigor of Shinan Pereira and the continued evolution and enhancement of Miyama Ryu. Perhaps through Mr. Rahming's efforts he will be known as the "Chronicler of the Lost Art".

Mr. Rahming's excellent style and method of catalouging the basics of the Miyama Ryu has allowed others to experience and understand the effectiveness of the technique. To those of us who are teachers, he inspires us to remain students true to our craft and continually seek to improve our technique. To the students he has helped to instill within many of them a desire to become teachers of the Ryu.

-**Demetrios Milliaressis**, October '92
Kaiden, Miyama Ryu Ju-jutsu

About the author

D'Arcy Rahming's martial arts credentials include Kaiden (Senior Instructor), red and white belt in Miyama Ryu Ju-jutsu, second degree black belt in Okinawan Goju Ryu Karate, and a first degree black belt in Judo. He has competed on an international level in Sport Karate.

Rahming has served as a consultant to police and federal agencies. He is the author of the books **Combat Ju-jutsu - The Lost Art** and **The College Student's Complete Guide to Self-Protection**, also published by Modern Bu-jutsu, Inc. Rahming currently teaches traditional martial arts and self-protection seminars to college students.

Introduction

In the early seventies four police officers were involved in a gunfight with two ex-convicts. Although the officers outnumbered the gunmen, they died from gunshot wounds. When the body of one of the dead officers, a rookie, was examined a large number of recently spent casings from his service revolver were found in his pockets. During the heat of battle he had wasted lifesaving moments collecting the casings and putting them into his pocket.

The police inquiry revealed that at the academy, police officers were required to pocket their spent casings between loadings when using the firing range so as not to leave a mess. Under the stress of a life-and-death situation, the rookie had automatically resorted to habits developed during training.

The idea that you will do exactly what you have been trained to do is the essence of combat Ju-jutsu. Combat Ju-jutsu is the modern version of classical Ju-jutsu, an ancient art of self-protection that contains among its weapons: methods of striking, kicking, throwing, joint locking and choking. The ability to perform any of these self-protection techniques in a fight is dependent on training as realistically as possible.

Combat Ju-jutsu requires an in-depth understanding of the modern street attack. All classical warrior arts and modern martial way differ from combat ju-jutsu because they do not easily provide answers for self-protection. Men no longer carry swords, which many of the classical schools still prepare students to defend against. The ritualism and sporting rules of the modern martial ways also present attacks that are different from the street.

Advanced Combat Ju-jutsu - Entrance to Secrets is based on the teachings of Antonio Pereira; he is the originator of the Miyama Ryu fighting system. This volume is intended for use as a reference for both beginning and advanced students of the Miyama Ryu as well as all martial artists interested in Ju-jutsu. The book elaborates on some of the aspects of combat Ju-jutsu that are integral to surviving a violent confrontation.

Shinan Pereira instinctively understood the need to teach his students methods of avoiding an attack that went beyond physical technique. While formulating the Miyama Ryu, he researched and evaluated how victims were attacked. The Miyama Ryu self-protection tactics are deeply rooted in the idea that practitioners must develop mental toughness, combat-effective body language and street smarts.

Miyama Ryu Ju-jutsu is by its nature in a constant state of refinement. The goal of the Miyama Ryu is that when future students and teachers of the art are called upon to defend their lives, their training will have adequately prepared them.

Classical Ju-jutsu

The samurai warriors of feudal Japan were the inventors of the deadly fighting techniques of classical Ju-jutsu. The warriors developed unarmed and short-arm techniques that could be used to incapacitate or kill an enemy when the warrior's primary weapon, usually the sword, was unavailable.

Ju-jutsu was not taught as a system separate from ken-jutsu (sword fighting) until 1532. A samurai, Takenouchi, formalized a subset of techniques for battle which he received in a vision after several days of austere training. Many other samurai Ju-jutsu schools soon developed.

Historically, the actual battlefield experience of classical Ju-jutsu teachers was transmitted through highly formalized prearranged fighting patterns. The scientific knowledge of the body's vital areas and balance points were acquired at the expense of lost limbs and lost lives. Techniques that did not work in combat remained with the bones of their creators, who died attempting them.

The classical Ju-jutsu as practiced by the samurai is almost extinct. Today, the term Ju-jutsu is lost to the Japanese public and survives mainly overseas. In Japan the techniques of classical Ju-jutsu did survive through the creation of new police and military arts. These new arts consist of Keijo-jutsu (medium- length stick), Taiho-jutsu (unarmed police arresting tactics), Keibo Soho (short truncheon), Tokusho Keibo Soho (collapsible truncheon), Hojo-jutsu (tying cord method), and Toshu Kakuto (military hand-to-hand combat).

Combat Ju-jutsu is a direct descendant of classical Ju-jutsu. The physical and mental principles of fighting learned from the feudal warriors are still valid today. But the final outcome between the two periods is different. The samurai warrior concentrated on killing his enemy, whereas the modern practitioner concentrates on doing whatever is reasonable to his enemy to avoid physical harm.

Classical Ju-jutsu is the parent art of Aikido, Judo and some styles of Karate. Some of the principles and training methods underlying the techniques that are propagated by these martial arts have proven useful to combat Ju-jutsu when put into the perspective of self-protection.

History of Miyama Ryu

In 1960 the Tremont School of Judo and Ju-jutsu opened its doors to the public for the first time. The founder, a fierce man named Antonio Pereira, taught a fighting style which he called Combato, the way of Combat.

Combato was a crude form of Ju-jutsu. The founder had learned these fighting techniques from commandos during World War II in Australia, where he had served as a sniper for the U. S. Army. He had supplemented this military hand-to-hand training with Judo.

In 1961, after a demonstration for a health club the founder was approached by a Japanese man, Nakabayashi. Nakabayashi, who was visiting the United States, was an instructor of Taiho-Jutsu (police arresting arts) and a seventh degree black belt in Kodokan Judo. He was impressed with Combato and encouraged the founder to travel to Japan to develop it further by training in more traditional arts.

At Nakabayashi's invitation, the founder traveled to Japan and studied martial arts for eight hours a day under such masters as Mifune of Judo and Ueshiba of Aikido. He lost more than 35 pounds in a six-month period. For his efforts, The founder was awarded a Nidan in Kodokan Judo and a teaching certificate in Aikido signed by Kisshomura Ueshiba.

The founder returned to the United States and began to teach Aikido at the Tremont School. But the Aikido wasn't suitable for the residents of the Bronx, who needed more aggressive self-defense techniques. He refined his original Combato, augmenting it with the classical techniques that he had learned. The founder called his method Miyama Ryu, which means the School of the Three Mountains, the English translation for Tremont and assumed the title of Shinan which means originator.

During the past 32 years, Miyama Ryu Ju-jutsu has become an international system. There are currently Miyama Ryu schools across the United States and in Santo Domingo, capital of the Dominican Republic. Miyama Ryu fighting techniques have been taught to U.S. Army Special Forces teams, Internal Revenue Service Criminal Investigation units, several police departments, and to thousands of civilians.

Interview with Shinan

Shinan, what influenced you to further your martial arts education in Japan?
I wanted to go to the Mecca, the birth place of the martial arts that I had grown to love. I felt the need to legitimatize myself since I was to pursue this as my life's work.

How does your Ju-jutsu differ?
The only arts that I teach in their pure forms are Aikido and Judo. I did not think that the classical arts, as they were practiced in Japan, were suited for self-defense. Although we use the classical techniques our applications are from the Western perspective. When you throw your arm at me, I'm going to break it if I can. I won't go into histrionics or wasted movements....I'm going to try to pull that arm out of the socket and shove it down your throat. That's the gist of my defenses.

Why do you abhor the use of the term master in the martial arts?
Ueshiba of Aikido was a master, Mifune of Judo was a master. I was privileged to have been touched by these men. I have studied martial arts for over 50 years and I do not consider myself a master. This rank inflation is why I chose to use classical titles instead of dan grades. Often people will try and compare a Miyama Ryu rank to a dan grade. To them I say there are no dan grade ranks in Miyama Ryu.

The Miyama Ryu technique appears very violent. Why is that?
People are always asking me 'Why is your approach so violent?' To which I reply, because they are violent to us!... If someone shouts at me, I do not respond. If someone swears at me, I do not respond. If someone calls my mother dirty names, I say thank-you very much. But when someone attacks me, then I respond.

Isn't training with this attitude dangerous?
Not at all, the classes are very controlled. Instructors must realize that a man may have to go to work the next day. If a man loses his job, he can lose his family so it is vital that instructors train with their students' safety foremost in mind.

Does size matter in Ju-jutsu?
All things being equal, a technically proficient big man can beat a technically proficient small man. But a good small man can beat a big man who has no technique.

What are your thoughts on carrying a weapon for self-defense?
Learn to use your natural weapons first. When you carry a knife, you become knifey; when you carry a stick, you become sticky; and when you carry a gun, you become gunny.

Interview with Shinan

What is your opinion of sport Ju-jutsu?
My first thoughts were, there's no such thing. Ju-jutsu fighting is often to the death. How can they have a competition in something like that. Then I found out that students were judged not on free fighting, but on how artistic and effective their techniques looked. Sport is not a direction I see for the Miyama Ryu.

Why did you offer a separate police tactics course?
The police have specialized needs for arresting, cuffing and controlling suspects. Topics such as gun retention are also addressed. Too often too much force is used because the officer has not been trained well-enough. Many corrections officers also use our methods because they have to operate unarmed.

Why is there not a children's group in Miyama Ryu?
A child should maintain his innocence. The Miyama Ryu is very harsh mentally and physically. A child cannot understand the severity of facing a knife, gun or a serious mugging.

You often call Ju-jutsu an insurance policy. Why is that?
I'm not a miracle maker. I don't say that the techniques will get you away scot-free. But what I try to do is to minimize the damage that a perpetrator will do to you. Usually when someone is angry at you, he'll get through and scratch you. I want that scratch to be a little less than mortal.

What should new students be prepared to do?
Take their time and learn their basics well. Everything in Miyama Ryu is step-by-step. You can't do rolls on day one and jump right into gun defenses. I'll answer any questions except 'what if?' I believe all 'what if' questions will be answered in time and with continued practice.

How does one become affiliated with the Miyama Ryu system of Ju-jutsu?
Over the years a lot of people have come to the Hombu Dojo in New York requesting to be graded in Ju-jutsu. Unfortunately, I have to tell these individuals that we're not in the business of handing out grades.... If you sincerely wish to be a part of the Miyama Ryu family, then come and train with us. If you are not near an affiliated school, then visit the Hombu Dojo or consider hosting or attending a seminar. I don't ask that you forget what you have learned previously, only that you put it aside for the time being and absorb what you can from the Miyama Ryu.

Zanshin (awareness)

A samurai warrior was prepared to face a violent attack at any time. The warriors called this heightened state of awareness "Zanshin". Miyama Ryu Ju-jutsu develops your Zanshin by providing you with steps that you can take which will increase your sense of awareness and develop your street smarts. These steps include adopting a readiness posture, developing your internal radar, nurturing good safety habits and identifying attacking patterns.

Your Zanshin makes you less likely to become a victim of a violent crime. Students of combat Ju-jutsu avoid many attacks by adopting a readiness posture. Your readiness posture in the dojo and on the street is a natural position. It signals to the attacker that you are alert and aware of your surroundings. In the readiness posture you walk or stand with your back straight and head up. Lean slightly forward, shifting your weight toward the balls of your feet. Your shoulders are relaxed and your hands hang loosely at your sides.

Zanshin develops your internal radar, your inner voice. The inner voice tells you "Something is wrong with this picture." Victims of crime often say that they felt something was not right just before the incident occurred but did not react to that feeling because they thought they might appear rude or that they were being paranoid.

Zanshin also requires you to cultivate good safety habits by taking crime prevention precautions. Again, think of the mind-set of a criminal. Who would you attack? A man who habitually approaches his apartment door keys in hand, and then turns 180 degrees before entering, or a man who approaches his apartment door, fumbles for his keys, and enters without so much as a glance over his shoulder?

Students of combat Ju-jutsu also learn to identify attacking patterns. For example, an adversary will naturally attempt to reduce his potential for being caught and incarcerated or even killed. Instinctively, he chooses a victim whom he perceives will put up the least resistance and is the most isolated, a target of opportunity.

Knowing this attack pattern you can circumvent it by not responding in a victim-like manner. If you are challenged, look the individual in the eye. Give short answers or say nothing. If he starts toward you, assume the readiness posture, extend a hand palm forward and tell him firmly to stop. Do not shuffle backward as this indecision may be taken as a sign of weakness. Any steps that you take should be very deliberate. If he doesn't stop, he may likely intend to assault you and you can react with whatever force is reasonable to subdue him.

Fudoshin (mind-set)

The warrior tried to face every life-threatening encounter with a clear and calm mind. He understood that how he managed his stress would be a big factor in determining if he lived or died. Developing a calm mind to manage stress was called "Fudoshin" by the classical warrior. Fudoshin is developed through four steps: understanding the effects of stress, breath control, nurturing your inner voice, and rehearsing mentally.

Everybody experiences stress to some degree in a fight. For example, hormones such as adrenalin rush into the blood stream. This rush is often termed the "startle response" or the "flight or fight syndrome." In this agitated state, as the blood rushes to your large muscles, movements that require small muscles become harder to execute. Techniques that could be performed easily in the dojo may become extremely difficult to execute.

Your ability to think analytically also diminishes. The stress of combat may cause you to overlook opportunities to escape a situation. Self-doubts may creep up. One common thought that occurs is "I can't believe this is happening to me!" Unfortunately, many people turn away, as if turning away will make the crisis disappear.

During a fight, time and perceptions become distorted. Many fights appear as if they are occurring in slow motion. Some police officers who survive gunfights have fired many more shots than they can remember discharging and many are unable to report parts of the altercation. Stress leads to tunnel vision, in which an individual focuses on a particular thing or adversary and disregards everything else.

Stress must be dealt with even after combat as the body returns gradually to its normal state. During this cool-down period, you may shake excessively or your voice may crack.

Breath control is the second phase of controlling stress. As the blood rush tightens your muscles, your throat may become constricted, causing you to fight for every breath. By breathing deeply from your abdomen you can minimize stress. In the Miyama Ryu, evasion and blocking techniques involve breathing in, while striking, throwing and joint breaking involve breathing out.

Nurturing your inner voice is the third component of Fudoshin. Your inner voice must override all your fears and reinforce positive ideas. "I will survive this conflict!" "I know exactly what I need to do!" "This is happening to me and I will deal with it right now!" You must repeat these type of thoughts to bolster your psyche and motivate you into action.

Mental rehearsal is the fourth tool for combatting stress. Imagine yourself in a crisis and create responses to it mentally. For example, the only reason a criminal attempts to isolate you from a group or to move you to a secondary scene is to make you even more vulnerable. If you are ever confronted with this dilemma and have rehearsed in your mind that this is the time you will fight, you will react without hesitation.

Kihon (basics)

Miyama Ryu Ju-jutsu is an eclectic system which has derived its techniques and training methods from classical Ju-jutsu, Karate, Judo, Aikido and western street style fighting. A Miyama Ryu Ju-jutsu response to a street attack may utilize techniques from any or all of the preceding arts. Techniques are learned in a formal manner first so that the students can better understand their underlying principles. The Miyama Ryu basics can be categorized as follows:

Taiso (Body conditioning)

Taiso involves preparing the body for a workout and cooling down the body after the workout. Taiso consists of aerobic and anaerobic exercises such as running, jumping jacks, groin and back stretches. The idea is that if the muscles and joints are loose there is less of a chance for minor injuries, such as a hamstring pull, during a workout. Routines will vary depending on the instructor. Note that all Miyama Ryu techniques can be performed without the benefit of a warmup as it is doubtful that your adversary will give you the benefit of a thirty minute warm up.

Ukemi (Break falls)

Ukemi, which involves basic falls and dramatic flips, is vital to the practice of Combat Ju-jutsu. In some of the more advanced Ju-jutsu techniques the student assuming the role of the attacker must survive a vicious fall while one or both of his limbs are being wrenched.

The Ukemi of the Miyama Ryu should be practiced on a matted surface. There will be occasions when a matted dojo is not available. In this case throws should be performed without taking the uke to the ground. Remember, when practicing, safety is the primary rule.

Atemi Waza (Striking techniques)

Atemi waza is used to unbalance or stun an adversary so that a throwing or joint-locking technique can be applied to him. Strikes are executed to vital areas of the body. Miyama Ryu Ju-jutsu incorporates Karate-jutsu's striking methods. Many other unorthodox striking methods are also used by the Miyama Ryu. For example, a head-butt might be used to disorient an adversary.

Kote Waza (Wrist technique)

Kote waza techniques are methods of dislocating the attacker's wrist as well as throwing him to the ground. The wrists are attacked with a twisting motion, both in the direction they naturally twist and the opposite direction. A Kote waza is always pre-empted by a striking technique aimed at distracting the adversary into loosening up his wrist by focusing on another area he believes is being more strenuously attacked.

Kihon (basics)

Kansetsu Waza (Joint-locking technique)

Kansetsu waza techniques are methods of fracturing an adversary's joint. Kansetsu waza is used as a major punishment technique against any attack and is extremely useful for in-close fighting where they may not be enough room to throw an attacker. Kansetsu waza is also preempted by a striking technique to loosen up the adversary.

Nage Waza (Throwing techniques)

Miyama Ryu utilizes Judo, Aikido and Classical Ju-jutsu throwing techniques. There are three principles involved in a good throw: unbalance, entrance, and execution.

All Miyama Ryu throws provide enough physical shock to the adversary's body so that he cannot continue to fight. Many of the responses use throws as the major component for punishing the adversary. Throwing an adversary to the ground also takes the fight out of him mentally and puts him on the defensive.

Shime Waza (Strangulation Techniques)

Circulatory and trachea strangulation techniques render an adversary unconscious in 5-20 seconds when applied. Trachea strangulations can cause severe damage to an adversary's throat. Circulatory strangulation that are used by Judo practitioners are also useful for self-defense. Strangulation techniques are not introduced until senior brown belt level in Miyama Ryu.

Osae-komi Waza (Ground controls)

Immobilization techniques (ground controls) are used to control an adversary once he has been thrown to the ground. They are normally a finishing response to Kansetsu waza and Kote waza techniques.

Tai-sabaki (Body positioning)

Tai-sabaki is the heart of combat Ju-jutsu. If you can't get out of the way of an attack, it won't matter how many strikes, throws or joint locks you know. In every Tai-sabaki movement, the adversary's intended target is moved out of striking range.

The Tai-sabaki movements were designed so that you could defend yourself from any direction that you move. Although the Tai-sabaki attacks are practiced against punches and pushes, they can also be practiced against grabs and kicks or any other kind of striking attack. In all situations after you have executed the Tai-sabaki and avoided the attack, you will be in a position to retaliate.

Taiso

Ukemi

Side fall

Bring your right leg forward. Bend your left knee and raise your right hand. Slap the ground. Tighten your abdomen by exhaling sharply. Land on your right side with your right hand striking the mat at a 45 degree angle and your left hand grasping your belt knot. Put your chin on your chest to protect your head against impact.

Rear fall

Raise your hands to shoulder height. Squat bending both knees. Throw yourself backwards. Tuck your chin to your chest to avoid hitting your head on the ground. Tighten your abdomen by exhaling. Slap the ground vigorously at a 45 degree angle. Land on your back exhaling sharply. Bring your knees up. If an adversary is standing over you it provides some protection.

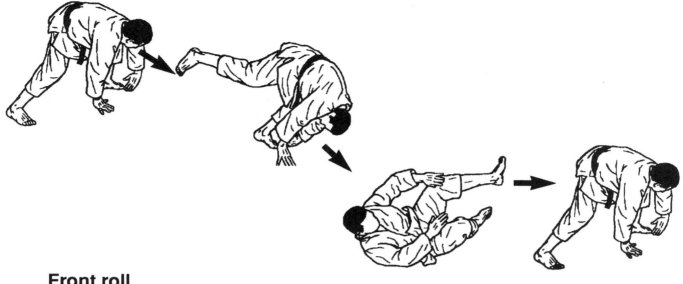

Front roll

Stand with your left foot forward, right hand touching the ground. Your left elbow should point in the direction of your roll. Push off with your feet and roll along your pinkie finger, your arm and diagonally across your back. Tuck your chin against your chest. At no point should your head touch the ground. As you roll tuck the trailing leg in and perform a complete arc with the lead leg. On completion of your roll you should return to the same position that you began with.

Free fall

Step forward with your right leg. Raise your right hand as high as you can towards the ceiling. Jump and somersault, bringing your right hand across your abdomen as if you are cutting yourself in half. Tuck your chin in. Slap the mat vigorously as you fall on your side. Tighten your abdomen and exhale on impact, so you do not have the wind knocked out of you.

Dead front fall

Jump up in the air and fall forward. Spread your legs apart in the air. Land on your forearms, palms of your hands and on the balls of your feet. Exhale sharply as you land and turn your head to either side to prevent smashing your nose.

Side separation fall

Bend both arms at the elbow and raise them palm facing outward. Leap forward and turn your hip so that your left leg crosses over your right. Land on your forearms and on the balls of your feet. Turn your head so that your face does not hit the ground. This fall should protect your face torso, groin and knees from impact.

Kote-gaeshi roll

Place the thumb of your left hand on the back of your right hand. Your fingers should wrap around the thumb side of your right palm. Push with your left hand and bend your wrist so that your palm is facing your bicep. Step forward with your right leg and place your bent wrist on the ground. Push off with your back leg and roll over your right shoulder and diagonally across your back. Return to your original standing position.

Aiki roll

Kneel on your left knee and place your left heel below your right buttock. Bend your wrists so that your fingers are cupped to the inside like a duck's beak. Touch both wrists to the ground. Push off of your legs, tuck your head and somersault. Return to your original position. This roll can be done from a standing position.

Somersault

Spread both feet about 1 1/2 times your shoulder width. Place both fists on the ground. Your hands should be at the same distance as your feet. Push off on both fists. Perform a somersault. Tuck your head in, do not let it touch the ground. On impact, tighten your abdomen and exhale sharply. Slap at 45 degrees with your hands. Arch your back so that the only parts of your body that make contact on impact are the balls of your feet, your shoulders and your palms. Your neck and head should not make contact with the ground. This fall can be performed with or without the hands used to slap out. As you become competent this technique can be accomplished from a forward somersault without putting your fists down.

Atemi Waza

Seiken (fore-fist)

Curl the fingers at the second joint. Then curl them again at the knuckles. Place your thumb over the fingers. This action makes a fist tight. Strike with the front two knuckles of the fore-fist.

Targets: face, chin, temple, ear, solar plexus, abdomen, ribs, groin, and kidney.

Uraken (back-fist)

Curl the fingers at the second joint. Then curl them again at the knuckles. Place your thumb over the fingers. This action makes a fist tight. Strike with the front two knuckles of the fore-fist.

Targets: face, chin, temple, ear, and nose

Empi (elbow)

Bend your arm at the elbow, so that your elbow is pointed towards the ground. Strike just above or below the point of the elbow.

Targets: Cheek, chin, side of the neck, rib cage, and spine.

Ude (forearm)

Bend your arm at the elbow, so that your elbow is pointed outward. Strike with the forearm.

Targets: Side of the neck, rib cage.

Shotei (heel palm)

Extend your fingers back and push your palm out. Bend your thumb and tuck it against your hand. The striking surface is the palm.
Targets: chin, temple, ear, solar plexus, ribs, spleen, groin.

Koko (web strike)

Open your hand. Squeeze your fingers together. Spread your thumb away from your hand. Bend your fingers as if you were holding a glass. Strike with the web of your hand.
Target: Throat

Haito (inner edge)

Open your hand. Squeeze your fingers together. Bend your thumb and tuck it against your palm. Strike with inner edge of the hand.
Targets: Between the upper lip and nose.

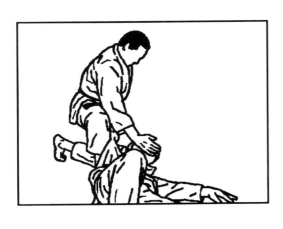

Shuto (knife edge)

Open your hand. Squeeze your fingers together. Bend your thumb and tuck it against the edge of your hand. Strike with outer edge of the hand.
Targets: nose, throat, collarbone, abdomen, ribs, spleen, groin.

Jo sokutei (ball of the feet)

Pull the toes back and bend the ankle forward. Strike with the ball of the foot.
Targets: shin, knee, groin, solar plexus, chin.

Ka sokutei (heel)

Push the heel outward and bend the ankle upwards. Strike with the bottom of the heel of the heel.
Targets: nose, jaw, solar plexus. solar plexus, groin.

Sokuto (side of the foot)

Pull the toes back and bend the ankle forward. Strike with the outer edge of the foot.
Targets: knee, groin, solar plexus, chin, throat.

Sokko (instep)

Pull the toes back and bend the ankle forward. Strike with the instep.
Targets: Cheek, lower rib cage, stomach.

Kote Waza

Kote-gaeshi 1

The adversary stands in a natural position with his hands at his side. Step forward with your left leg so that your toes are about the same level as the heel of his right foot. Reach down with your left hand and grab the adversary's right hand by placing your thumb on the back of his hand and placing your fingers over the thumb side. Bring your right hand to meet your left hand, thumbs crossing on the back. Turn his fingers up towards the ceiling bending his wrist towards his bicep. Keep your wrist waist high. Step in and place your right leg behind his right leg. Turn his wrist towards his thumb. This action will break his wrist and throw him to his back.

Safety considerations: Uke must take a back fall.

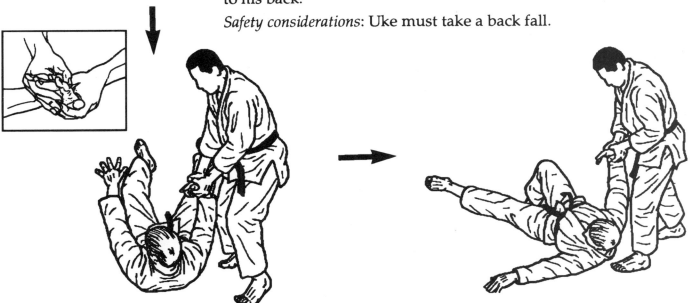

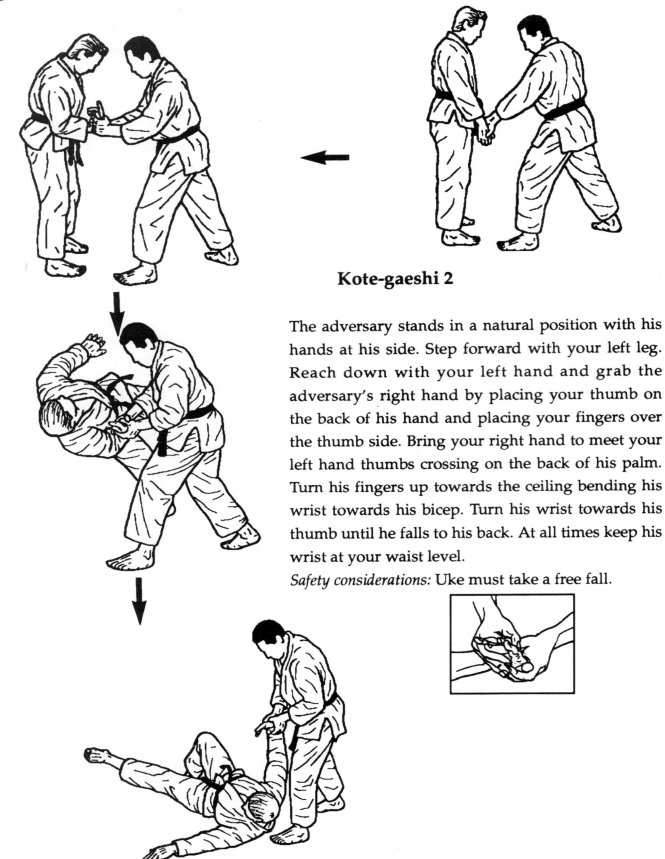

Kote-gaeshi 2

The adversary stands in a natural position with his hands at his side. Step forward with your left leg. Reach down with your left hand and grab the adversary's right hand by placing your thumb on the back of his hand and placing your fingers over the thumb side. Bring your right hand to meet your left hand thumbs crossing on the back of his palm. Turn his fingers up towards the ceiling bending his wrist towards his bicep. Turn his wrist towards his thumb until he falls to his back. At all times keep his wrist at your waist level.

Safety considerations: Uke must take a free fall.

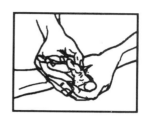

Kote-gaeshi 3

The adversary stands in a natural position with his hands at his side. Step forward with your left leg. Reach down with your left hand and grab the adversary's right hand by placing your thumb on the back of his hand and placing your fingers over the thumb side. Turn his fingers up towards the ceiling bending his wrist towards his bicep. Bring your right hand to meet your left hand so that your thumbs cross on the back of his hand. Step in with your right foot and then pivot 90-180 degrees away from him counter clockwise on your right leg. Turn his wrist towards his thumb until he falls to his back. At all times keep his wrist at your waist level.

Safety considerations: Uke must take a free fall.

Kotegaeshi 4

The adversary stands in a natural position with his hands at his side. Step forward with your left leg. Reach down with your left hand and grab the adversary's right hand by placing your thumb on the back of his hand and placing your fingers over the thumb side. Turn his fingers up towards the ceiling bending his wrist towards his bicep. Bring your right hand to meet your left hand so that your thumbs cross on the back of his hand. Step in with your right foot and then pivot 90- 180 degrees away from him counter clockwise on your right foot to a left kneeling position. Your right knee should be in front of his leg. Turn his wrist towards his thumb until he falls to his back. At all times keep his wrist at your waist level.

Safety considerations: Uke must take a free fall.

Kote-gaeshi 5

The adversary stands in a natural position with his hands at his side. Step forward with your left leg. Reach down with your left hand and grab the adversary's right hand by placing your thumb on the back of his hand and placing your fingers over the thumb side. Turn his fingers up towards the ceiling bending his wrist towards his bicep. Bring your right hand to meet your left hand so that your thumbs cross on the back of his hand. Step in with your right foot and then pivot 90- 180 degrees away from him counter clockwise on your right leg to a kneeling position. Extend your right leg, heel up, and throw the adversary over your right leg. Turn his wrist towards his thumb until he falls to his back. At all times keep his wrist at your waist level.

Safety considerations: Uke must take a free fall. The knee of your extended leg must point towards the ground so that if the adversary falls on it, it will not become dislocated.

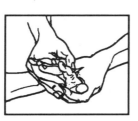

Kote-gaeshi 6

The adversary stands in a natural position with his hands at his side. Step forward with your left leg. Reach down with your left hand and grab the adversary's right hand by placing your thumb on the back of his hand and placing your fingers over the thumb side. Turn his fingers up towards the ceiling bending his wrist towards his bicep. Step in with your right foot and strike Shuto to his neck with your right hand. Turn his wrist towards his thumb as you pivot 90- 180 degrees away from him counter clockwise on your right leg. Break the adversary's wrist and continue to maintain pressure on the adversary's head as you throw him to his back. Keep his wrist at your waist height at all times. Once he starts to fall both hands go to his wrist.
Safety considerations: Uke must take a free fall.

Kote-gaeshi 7

The adversary stands in a natural position with his hands at his side. Step forward with your left leg. Reach down with your left hand and grab the adversary's right hand by placing your thumb on the back of his hand and placing your fingers over the thumb side. Turn his fingers up towards the ceiling bending his wrist towards his bicep. Step in with your right foot and strike Shuto to his wrist with your right hand. Turn his wrist towards his thumb as you pivot 90- 180 degrees away from him counter clockwise on your right leg. Break the adversary's wrist as you throw him to his back. Keep his wrist at your waist height at all times. Once he starts to fall both hands go to his wrist.
Safety considerations: Uke must take a free fall.

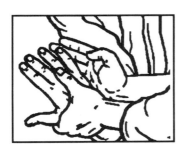

Kote-gaeshi 8

The adversary stands in a natural position with his hands at his side. Step forward with your left leg. Reach down with your left hand and grab the adversary's right hand by placing your thumb on the back of his hand and placing your fingers over the thumb side. Turn his fingers up towards the ceiling bending his wrist towards his bicep. Reach in underneath the adversary's elbow with your right hand and grab his right hand with your fingers placed on the back of hand. Step in with your right leg, pivot on your right foot, plant your left leg and block the adversary's right ankle with your right foot. Break the adversary's wrist and throw the adversary over your extended leg.

Safety considerations: Uke must take a free fall. Note that your knee is pointed down so that if the adversary falls awkwardly on your knee he will not dislocate it.

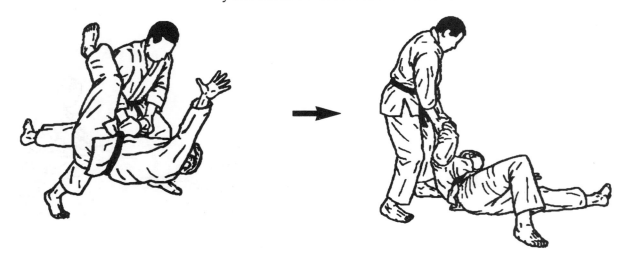

Advanced Combat Ju-jutsu **Pg 39**

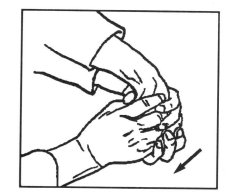

Compound Kote-gaeshi

Block the adversary's punch with your left hand and then grab his wrist. Redirect his arm forward across the front of your body. Bring your left hand to meet your right with your thumbs crossed on the back of his hand. Pivot on your left foot and step back with your right leg and duck under his arm. Twist his wrist towards the thumb and kneel down. This action will break his wrist and throw him to the ground.

Safety considerations: Uke must take a free fall.

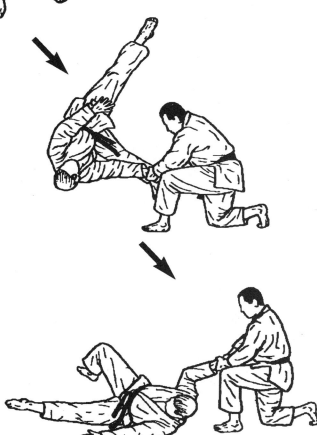

Shiho-nage

Block the adversary's punch with your left hand and then grab his wrist. Bring your right hand to meet your left with your thumbs crossed on the back of his hand. Redirect his hand forward across the front of your body. Step forward slightly with your left leg and twist your hips 180 degrees away from him as you slide under his outstretched hand. Bend his arm at the elbow. His wrist is now facing his bicep. Pull his hand down towards you violently and dislocate his wrist and shoulder as you throw him to his back.

Safety considerations: Pull the Uke firmly but gently to avoid dislocation.

Pendulum

The adversary stands in a natural position with his hands at his side. Step forward with your right leg and grab the adversary's right hand with your right hand. Your thumb should be on the back of his hand and your fingers are draped over the knife edge of his hand. Bring your left hand to meet your right hand fingers crossed on the back of the adversary's hand. Step back with your right leg and whip the adversary's hand in a clockwise direction so that his fingers are pointing towards the ceiling hand pressed towards the adversary's head. This action will shatter the adversary's wrist and make him bend over at the waist. Push the damaged wrist towards his head and the adversary will fall to the ground in a front fall.

Safety considerations: The Uke should go with the pendulum motion to avoid having his wrist dislocated.

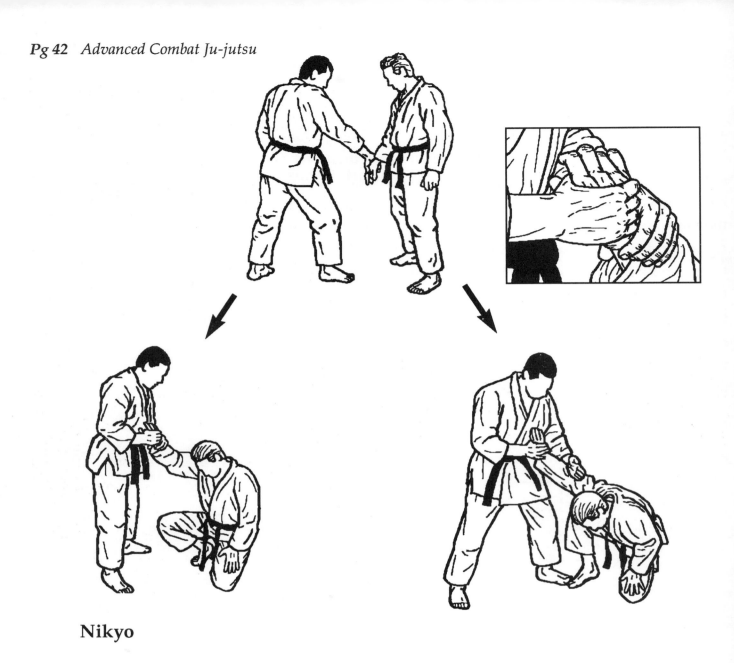

Nikyo

The adversary stands in a natural position with his hands at his side. Step forward with your right leg and grab the adversary's right hand with your right hand. Your thumb should be on the back of his hand and your fingers are draped over the knife edge of his hand. Step back with your right leg. Bring the back of his fingers to your sternum locking his hand against your chest. Keep his elbow slightly bent. Dislocate the adversary's wrist. Straighten his arm and place your hand on his elbow. Bring him to his face.

Forearm: Strike the top of his forearm near his elbow with your left hand and twist the knife edge of his right hand towards his body with your right hand. Dislocate the adversary's wrist. Keep the adversary's elbow bent slightly.

Safety considerations: Apply pressure gradually to avoid dislocating the Uke's wrist.

Sankyo

Block the adversary's right round house punch with your left hand. Step in with your right leg and strike to the bend in the adversary's arm. Push his right arm up so that his elbow is pointing towards the ceiling. Pivot 180 degrees under his arm on your right foot, twisting his wrist with both hands keeping the elbow up perpendicular to the floor.

Kansetsu waza basic: Pull his hand in front of you and apply Waki-gatame.

Throw: Step in front of him with your left leg and swing your hands in arc. This action will dislocate the adversary's wrist and throw him to the ground.

Seoi nage: Pivot into a shoulder throw after breaking the wrist. In class be sure to release the pressure on the uke's wrist before you throw.

Safety considerations: Simulate the breaking of the wrist in class. Uke should slap his body repeatedly to indicate that technique has been effectively applied.

Variation 1

Variation 2

Kote waza controls

The adversary stands in a natural position with his hands at his side. Step forward with your left leg so that your toes are at the same level as his heels. Grab the back of his right elbow with your left hand thumb up. Pivot 180 degrees clockwise on the ball of your left foot. Grab his right hand with your right hand. Your fingers should be on the back of his hand. Bring your left hand to meet your right hand crossing your fingers on the back of his hand. Bend the adversary's arm at his elbow by bringing the adversary's hand up. The adversary's elbow should rest against your sternum. Bend his wrist towards his body with his fingers pointing downwards.

Variation 1: Apply pressure with his palm up, pulling the wrist towards you.

Variation 2: Apply pressure pulling down on the fingers with his palm up.

Safety considerations: This is a pain compliance technique. But the pressure can dislocate the adversary's wrist if done aggressively.

Kansetsu waza

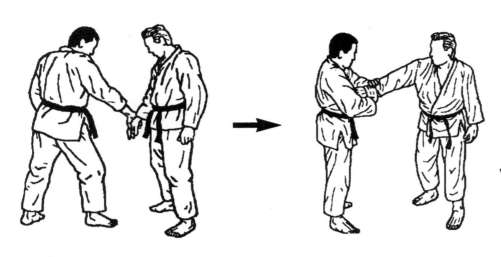

Kansetsu waza basic (Waki-gatame)

The adversary stands in a natural position with his hands at his side. Step forward with your right leg and grab the adversary's right wrist with your thumbs pointing down. Bring your left hand to meet your right hand fingers crossed on the adversary's wrist. Stepping back on your right leg. Step in front of the adversary's right foot with your left foot while dropping into a modified horse stance. Keep your back straight and do not bend forward at the waist. Brace down with your armpit on the adversary's elbow. Simultaneously, pull his wrist upward. Exhale and tighten your abdomen. This action will compound fracture the adversary's elbow. Bring the adversary down to the ground by stepping your left leg across your right, while applying pressure with your left palm on the compound fracture. Continue to apply pressure on the elbow with your left hand as right hand holds his wrist up at your knee.

Safety considerations: Simulate the break in class. Uke should bend forward to alleviate any pressure, and signal submission by slapping his side or the mat.

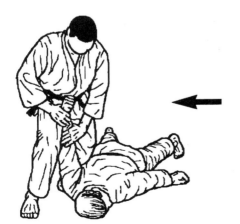

Waki-gatame with wrist pressure

The adversary stands in a natural position with his hands at his side. Step forward with your right leg and grab the adversary's right wrist with your thumbs pointing down. Bring your left hand to meet your right hand fingers crossed on the adversary's wrist. Stepping back on your right leg. Step in front of the adversary's right foot with your left foot while dropping into a modified horse stance. Keep your back straight and do not bend forward at the waist. Brace down with your armpit on the adversary's elbow. Simultaneously, pull his wrist upward. Exhale and tighten your abdomen. This action will compound fracture the adversary's elbow. Apply pressure to the wrist by pressing it towards his head. Bring him down and kneel on his shoulder blade as you continue to apply pressure to his wrist.

Safety considerations: Simulate the break in class. Uke should bend forward to alleviate any pressure, and signal submission by slapping his side or the mat.

Ude-garami

The adversary throws a right punch as he steps forward with his right leg. Step forward with your left leg and block the punch and strike at his face. Grab his right hand at the wrist with your left hand. Reach over his elbow and grab your right wrist with your right hand. Pivot 180 degrees clockwise on the ball of your left foot twisting the adversary's arm behind his back. The adversary will bend forward. Continue your pivot and bring him to the ground face first.

Safety considerations: Uke should go with the twisting motion. When the adversary is down apply pressure gradually. Uke should slap when he is on the ground to signal submission.

Hammerlock

As the adversary attacks with a looping right roundhouse punch, step forward into a left front stance. Inhale sharply and execute a left sided block to his forearm. Immediately strike to the crook of his elbow and push up with the knife edge of your right hand to form a bridge. Step under the bridge with your right leg, pivot on your right counter clockwise. Pull and twist the adversary's arm behind him with your left hand. Trap the adversary's wrist in the crook of your right elbow. Dislocate his right shoulder by driving your right arm up and grabbing his collar. Grab the adversary's hair to control his head and hold him in this manner.

Safety considerations: Apply pressure gradually on the hammerlock. Forceful movements will cause dislocation. Uke should slap the side of his body to indicate submission.

Devil's handshake

Block the adversary's right roundhouse punch with your left hand. Step across his body with your left leg and redirect his arm to your right hand. Pull his hand forward across the front of your body. Turn his wrist towards his thumb and reach up and place your left hand behind his neck by sliding your arm under his outstretched arm. Pull down fracturing his elbow across your bicep.

With clothing: Reach up and place your left hand on his left collar by sliding your arm under his outstretched arm. Turn his wrist towards his thumb and pull down fracturing his elbow across your bicep.

Safety considerations: Apply pressure against the elbow slowly to avoid injury when simulating the break. Uke should slap the side of his body repeatedly to indicate submission.

Arm bars

The adversary throws a right roundhouse punch at you. Step across his body with your left leg and redirect his arm to your right hand. Pull his hand forward across the front of your body as you step underneath. Place his elbow against the top of your left shoulder. Pull down sharply and across your body dislocating the adversary's elbow.

Variations: This armbar can also be done against the top of your other shoulder or the crook of your elbow.

Safety considerations: Apply pressure against the elbow slowly to avoid injury when simulating the break. The Uke should slap the side of his body repeatedly when signalling submission.

Tigerlock

Stand in a natural position facing adversary. As the adversary attacks with a looping right step forward and execute a circular block. Encircle his right arm with your left arm so that his elbow is trapped just below the crook of your arm. Stop his forward motion by placing your hand on his shoulder. Grab your right wrist with your left hand as you grab his throat with a Koko. Pull up with your forearm and compound fracture the adversary's elbow.
Safety considerations: Simlulate the break in class. Uke should slap the side of his body to indicate submission when he feels the joint-lock.

Kansetsu waza controls

Execute a circular block against the adversary's right roundhouse punch. Take a step in front of him with your left leg as you redirect the adversary's hand across your body. Encircle his arm, trapping his elbow, with your left arm and grab your right arm. Fracture his elbow across your forearm.
Variation: Grab your own lapel to tighten the lock.
Safety considerations: Simulate the break in class. Uke should slap the side of his body to indicate submission.

Nage Waza

Ju-jutsu Seoi nage

Ippon Seoi nage

Grab the adversary formally on the right side. Step diagonally across with your right foot to the inside of his feet. Capture the Uke's armpit in the bend of your right elbow making a fist with your right hand. Pivot on your right foot, bringing your left foot in parallel. In order to gain leverage your waist should be below the adversary's waist. Bend forward at the waist draping the adversary onto your back. Pull him down to your left as you look to the left. Spring up with your legs, rotate your shoulders and throw the Uke over your back.

Ju-jutsu Seoi nage: Place his elbow against the top of your left shoulder. Pull down sharply and across your body dislocating the adversary's elbow and throwing him to his back.

Safety considerations: Do not complete Ju-jutsu Seoi nage in class to prevent injuries. The Uke must slap the side of his body to signal submission.

Koshi-guruma

Grab the Uke formally on his right side. Step diagonally across with your right foot inside of his feet. Pull the Uke's right arm at the elbow and unbalance him to his right front corner. Reach around and grab the Uke's neck with your arm making a tight fist. Pivot on your right foot, bringing your left foot parallel to your right. Your waist should be lower than your adversary's waist. Bend at the waist draping the adversary onto your back. Pull him to your left and look left so he rolls over your hip and not your head.

Uki otoshi

Start in a formal position. Step back with your left leg. Pull the adversary towards you with both hands and break his balance forward. Pivot 90 degrees counterclockwise. Drop to your right knee. Continue to pull the adversary's right arm between his legs forming a full circle.

Osoto-gari

Start in a formal position. Step in with your left foot and off-balance the Uke to his right rear corner by turning your arms in a circular fashion. You should make contact chest to chest. Bring your right leg forward and reapthe Uke's right leg, your toes pointed down. The adversary will be thrown to his back.

Ju-jutsu Osoto-gari: Drive your heel into his achilles tendon as you throw him to his back. Traditionally the Samurai wore wooden shoes (geta).

Ju-jutsu Osoto-gari

Pg 56 Advanced Combat Ju-jutsu

Sukuinage

Start in a formal position. Step to his left side with your right foot. Bring your left foot to meet your right foot, then step behind the adversary with your right. At all times maintaining your hold on his right elbow. He is now unbalanced to the rear over your right leg. Your right hand is straight across his body at his waist. Once unbalanced grab behind the adversary's knees, pick him up and throw him with your body. As the Uke falls step back with your right foot.

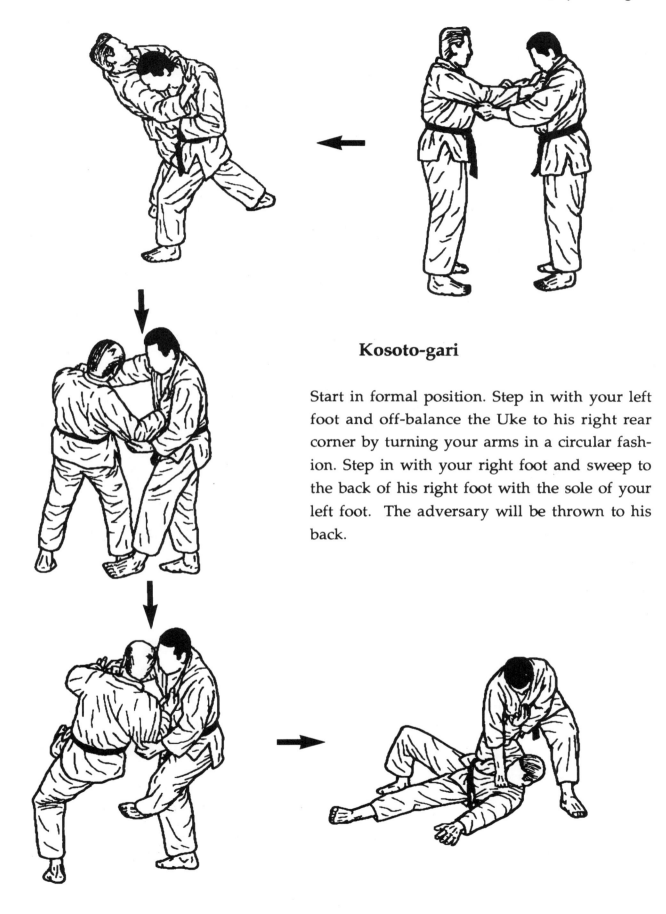

Kosoto-gari

Start in formal position. Step in with your left foot and off-balance the Uke to his right rear corner by turning your arms in a circular fashion. Step in with your right foot and sweep to the back of his right foot with the sole of your left foot. The adversary will be thrown to his back.

O goshi

Grab the Uke formally on his right side. Step diagonally across with your right foot inside of his feet. Pull the Uke's right arm at the elbow and unbalance him to his right front corner. Reach around and grab the Uke's waist. Pivot on your right foot, bringing your left foot in parallel to your right. Your waist should be lower than your adversary's waist. Bend at the waist draping the adversary onto your back. Pull him down to your left and look left so he rolls over your hip and not your head.

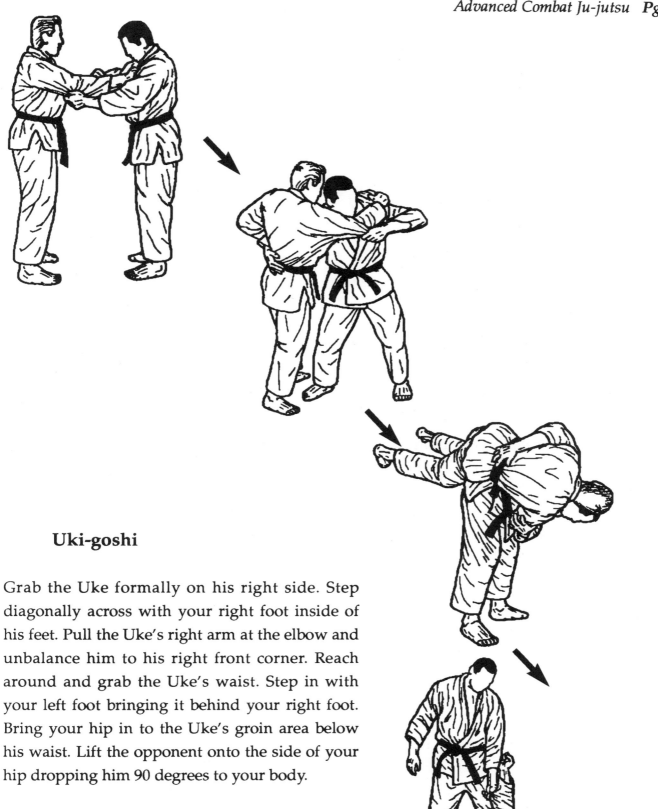

Uki-goshi

Grab the Uke formally on his right side. Step diagonally across with your right foot inside of his feet. Pull the Uke's right arm at the elbow and unbalance him to his right front corner. Reach around and grab the Uke's waist. Step in with your left foot bringing it behind your right foot. Bring your hip in to the Uke's groin area below his waist. Lift the opponent onto the side of your hip dropping him 90 degrees to your body.

Pg 60 Advanced Combat Ju-jutsu

Ju-jutsu tai-otoshi

Start in a formal position. Step diagonally across with your right foot. Pull the adversary's right arm at the elbow. This action will unbalance him to his right front corner. Step in with your left foot behind your right foot outside your Uke's left foot. Pivot onto your left knee and extend your right foot blocking his right ankle. You should be on the ball of your foot with your heel pointing upward. Your knee should be pointing downwards to avoid dislocation should the adversary fall on your knee. Turn your head away from the adversary as you push and pull your arms as if using a bow and arrow. Straighten your right leg under your opponents knee causing him to go up on his toes and fall forward.

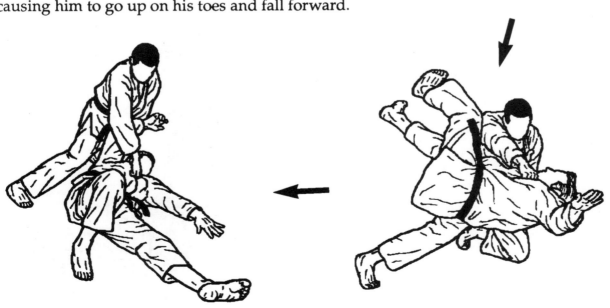

Ju-jutsu Harai-goshi

Harai-goshi

Start in formal position with your right hand grabbing the adversary's collar behind his neck. Step diagonally across with your right foot. Pull the adversary's right arm forward at the elbow. Lift up on his collar, at the same time turn the knife edge of both hands towards the sky. This action will unbalance him to his right front corner. Step in with your left foot behind your right foot. Bend at the waist and reap the adversary with your right leg. Pull to your left and look to your left. Start the reap below his right knee. Throw the adversary to his back.

Ju-jutsu Harai-goshi: Start the reap below the side of his right knee. This reap will dislocate the adversary's knee.

Safety considerations: When practicing Ju-jutsu Harai-goshi reap at the thigh to avoid dislocating the adversary's knee.

Judo tai-otoshi

Start in formal position. Step diagonally across with your right foot. Pull the adversary's right arm at his elbow. This action will unbalance him to his right front corner. Step in with your left foot behind your right foot outside your Uke's left foot. Pivot and extend your right foot blocking his right ankle. You should be on the ball of your foot with your heel pointing upwards. Your knee should be pointing downwards to avoid dislocation should the adversary fall on your knee. Turn your head away from the adversary as you push and pull your arms as if using a bow and arrow. Straighten your right leg under your adversary's knee causing him to go up on his toes and fall forward.

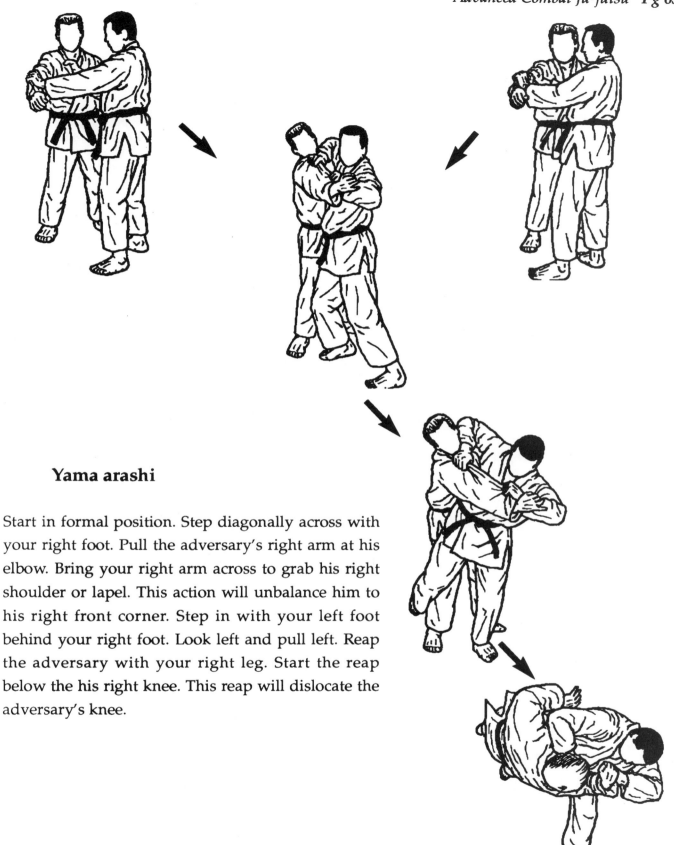

Yama arashi

Start in formal position. Step diagonally across with your right foot. Pull the adversary's right arm at his elbow. Bring your right arm across to grab his right shoulder or lapel. This action will unbalance him to his right front corner. Step in with your left foot behind your right foot. Look left and pull left. Reap the adversary with your right leg. Start the reap below the his right knee. This reap will dislocate the adversary's knee.

Pg 64 Advanced Combat Ju-jutsu

Ju-jutsu Ouchi-gari

Ouchi-gari

Start in formal postion. Step forward with your left leg and pull the adversary around to your right side so that he takes a big step, by pulling down with your right hand and pushing with your left hand. This action will immobilize his feet so that he cannot step back with his right leg or raise his left to block your throw. Insert your right leg between his legs and make a semi circle behind his left leg. Throw him to his back.

Ju-jutsu Ouchi-gari: Insert your right leg between his legs and entagle his right leg. When you throw him to the ground his knee will become dislocated.

Safety considerations: Do not take the Uke to the ground with this technique to avoid knee dislocation.

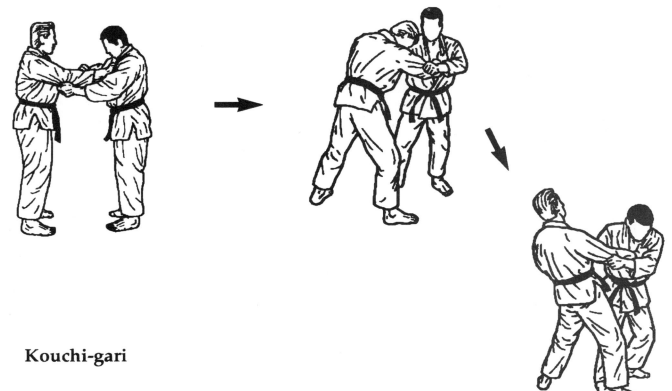

Kouchi-gari

Start in formal position. Step back in a semicircle with your left leg and pull the adversary so that he takes a big step forward with his right leg. Pull down with your right hand and forward with your left hand. This action will immobilize his feet so that he cannot step back with his left leg or raise his right leg to block the throw. Insert your right leg between his legs and make a semi circle behind his right foot. Sweep his heel with the bottom of your foot and throw the adversary to his back.

Morote Seoi nage

Start in formal position. Step diagonally across with your right foot. Turn the back of your left hand toward the sky as you pull the adversary forward. Drive your right elbow into the adversary's right armpit. Pivot on your right foot and bring your left foot in so that your back is to the adversary's front. Both feet should be between his feet. In order to gain leverage your waist should be below his waist. Drape the man on your back by leaning forward. Look left and pull left, throwing him to his back.

Safety considerations: Your wrist must be bent forward when executing the throw.

Tomoe Nage

Start in formal position. Unbalance the adversary forward by pulling forward and turning the knife edge of both hands towards the sky. Fall to your back and slide your hips between the adversary's legs. If you do not slide your hips in, your throw will be easily blocked by the adversary leaning forward. Place your foot in the adversary's abdomen and throw him over your head.

Ju-jutsu Tomoe Nage: Kick him in the groin and throw him over your head.

Ju-jutsu Tomoe Nage

Uki waza

Start in formal position. Step back with your left leg. Unbalance the adversary forward by pulling forward and turning the knife edge of both hands towards the sky. Fall to your left side and slide your hips between the adversary's legs. Extend your left leg blocking his right leg. Turn your arms in a wide circle counter clockwise. Throw the adversary over your left shoulder.

Safety considerations: Release the Uke so that he takes a roll. Holding onto him could possibly cause his shoulder to become dislocated.

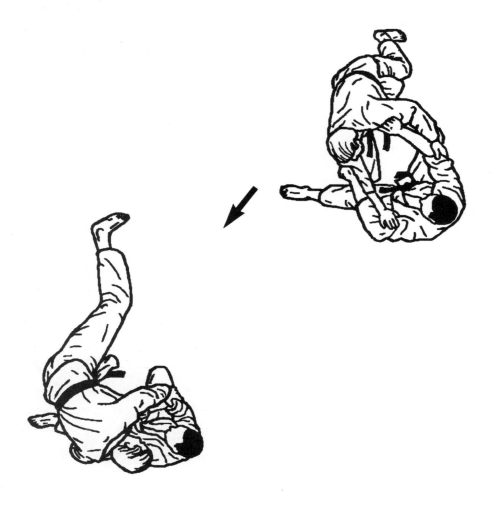

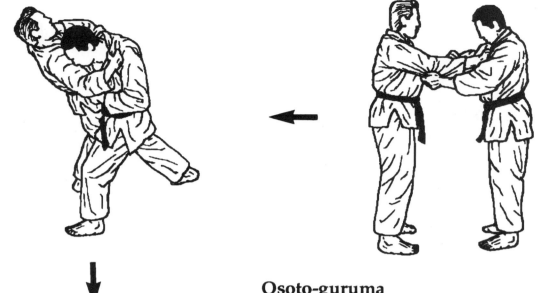

Osoto-guruma

Start in formal position. Take a big step forward with your left leg and break the adversary's balance to his right rear corner by keeping him close to your chest. Bring your right leg forward and reap both of the adversary's legs. He will be thrown to his back.

Ju-jutsu Osoto-guruma: Drop to your left knee and extend your right leg heel up behind his leg. Pull down and slam the adversary to the ground onto his back.

Ju-jutsu Osoto-guruma

Kata-guruma

Start in a formal position. Step diagonally across with your right foot. Pull the adversary's right arm at his elbow. Lift up on the lapel turning the knife edge of both hands towards the sky. This action will unbalance him to his right front corner. Grab inside the adversary's right knee with your right hand. Drape the adversary across your shoulders and bring your left foot to your right foot until your feet are shoulder width apart. Throw him on his back to your left front corner.

Ju-jutsu Sode tsuri komi-goshi

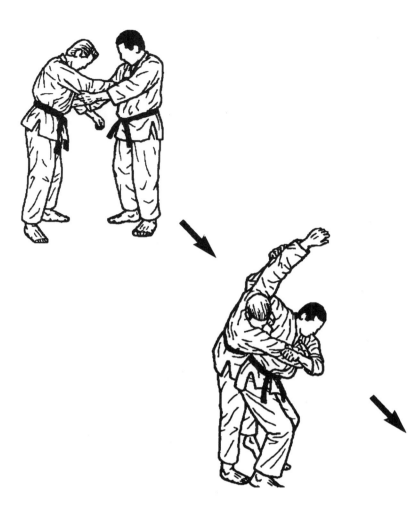

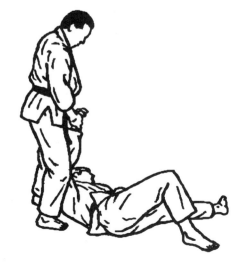

Sode tsuri komi-goshi

Start in a formal position. Step diagonally across with your right foot. Pull the adversary's right arm at his elbow. Lift up on his right elbow by turning the knife edge of your left hand towards the sky. This action will unbalance him to his right front corner. With your right hand grab under his leftt sleeve. Push up on his left sleeve with your elbow to the outside. Step in with your left foot so that both feet are between his feet. Drape the adversary onto your back. Pull him to your left and look to your left so that he rolls over your back and not your head.

Ju-jutsu Sode tsuri komi-goshi: Execute a right elbow strike into the adversary's chin.

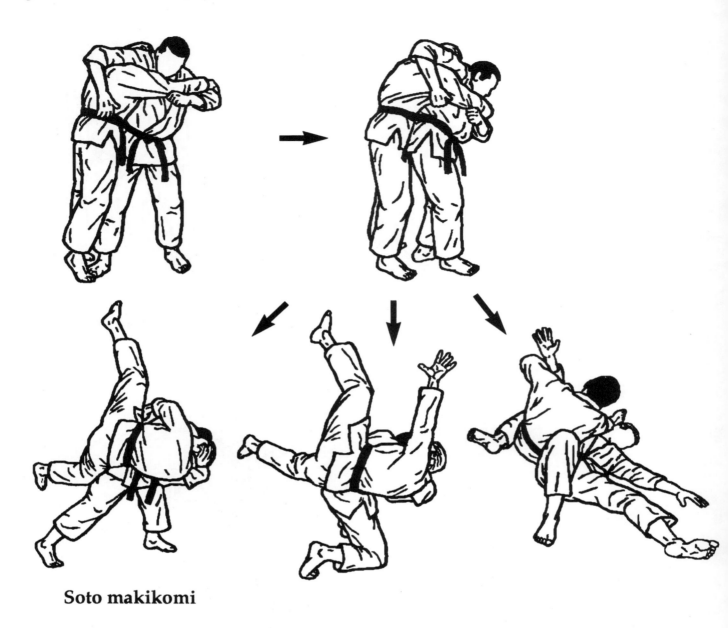

Soto makikomi

Start in formal position. Step diagonally across with your right foot. Pull the adversary's right arm at his elbow. Lift up on his right elbow by turning the knife edge of your left hand towards the sky. Stretch your right hand over the adversary's right shoulder and clamp down with your elbow pulling him to you. Your right chest should be against his right chest. Step in with your left foot so that both feet are between his feet. Drape the adversary onto your back. Reap below his knee.

Stage 1: Extend the right leg all the way back and allow the adversary to fall to his side. Pull him to your left and look to your left so that he rolls over your back and not your head.

Stage 2: Extend the right leg all the way back then drop to your right knee and pull him to your left and look to your left so that he rolls over your back and not your head.

Stage 3: Execute an aggressive side fall and land on the adversary's side. This fall will crush the adversary's ribs.

Tsuri-goshi

Start in formal position. Step diagonally across with your right foot. Pull the adversary's right arm at his elbow. Lift up on his right elbow by turning the knife edge of your left hand towards the sky. This action will unbalance him to his right front corner. Step in with your left foot so that both feet are between his feet. Reach behind and grab the adversary's belt. Drape the adversary onto your back. Pull up on his belt with your right hand as you pull him to your left with your left hand. Look to your left so that he rolls over your back and not your head.

Pg 74 Advanced Combat Ju-jutsu

Ju-jutsu Hane-goshi

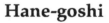

Hane-goshi

Start in a formal position and grab the adversary's collar behind the neck. Step diagonally across with your right foot. Pull the adversary's right arm at his elbow. Lift up on the collar turning the knife edge of both hands towards the sky. This action will unbalance him to his right front corner. Step in with your left foot behind your right foot. Bend at the waist and reap the adversary with your right leg. Both feet should be inside the adversary's feet. Bend your right knee and drive the knife edge of your right foot into the side of the adversary's shin. Throw the adversary to his back.

Ju-jutsu Hane-goshi: Drive the knife edge of your right foot into the side of the adversary's groin while you are still pulling up.

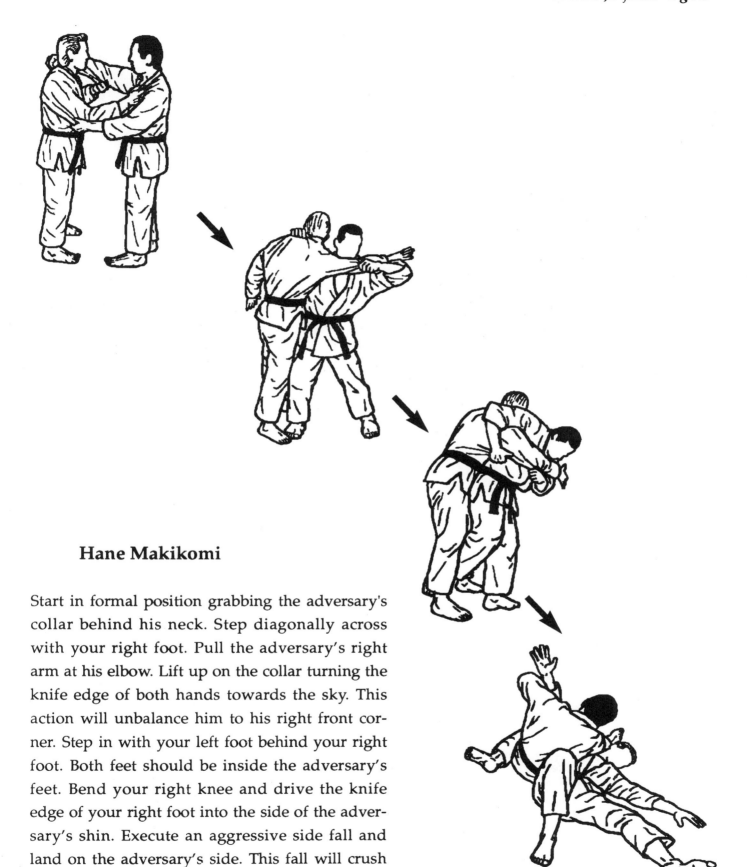

Hane Makikomi

Start in formal position grabbing the adversary's collar behind his neck. Step diagonally across with your right foot. Pull the adversary's right arm at his elbow. Lift up on the collar turning the knife edge of both hands towards the sky. This action will unbalance him to his right front corner. Step in with your left foot behind your right foot. Both feet should be inside the adversary's feet. Bend your right knee and drive the knife edge of your right foot into the side of the adversary's shin. Execute an aggressive side fall and land on the adversary's side. This fall will crush the adversary's ribs.

Pg 76   Advanced Combat Ju-jutsu

Uchi mata

Start in formal position. Step diagonally across with your right foot. Pull the adversary's right arm at his elbow. Lift up on the collar while turning the knife edge of both hands towards the sky. This action will unbalance him to his right front corner. Step in with your left foot behind your right foot. Both feet should be inside the adversary's feet. Bend at the waist and reap the adversary's inner thigh with your right leg. Pull to the left and look to the left. Throw the adversary to his back.

Hiza Guruma

Start in formal position. Step with your right leg to the left side of adversary's body. Pull the adversary up and forward by turning the knife edge of both hands towards the sky. Place the sole of your left foot on the right side of the adversary's right knee. Pivot 180 degrees counter-clockwise on the ball of your right foot. Turn your hands as if you were turning a steering wheel. Collapse the adversary's knee and throw him to his back.

Sasae tsurikomi ashi

Start in formal postion. Step with your right leg to the left side of adversary's body. Pull the adversary up and forward by turning the knife edge of both hands towards the sky. Place the sole of your left foot at the bottom of his shin bone. Pivot 180 degrees counter clockwise on the ball of your right foot. Turn your hands as if you were turning a steering wheel. Throw the adversary to his back.

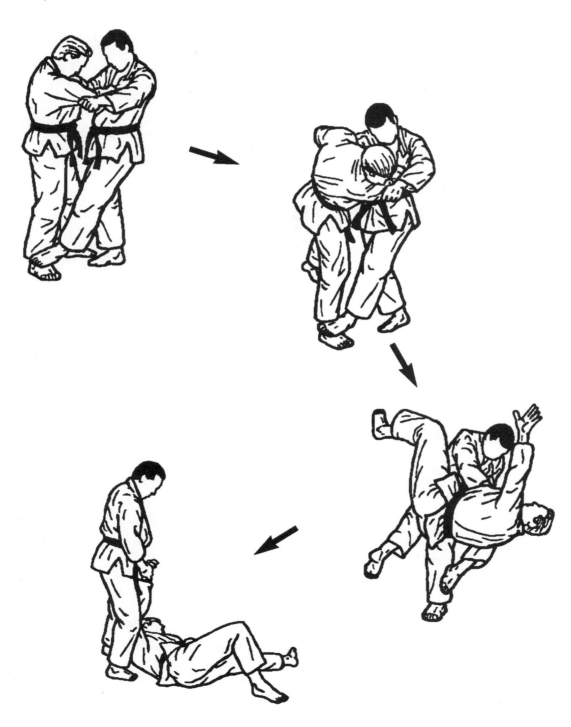

Ushiro goshi

The adversary attempts Koshi-guruma. Squat to lower your center of gravity and push up with your left hand on the adversary's right elbow as he attempts to entrap your neck. Place your left hand on the small of the adversary's back, fingers down. Tighten your abdomen, and pull the adversary to you so that his hips are just above your waist. Exhale and pick the adversary up. Turn him to his left side and throw him to his left side.

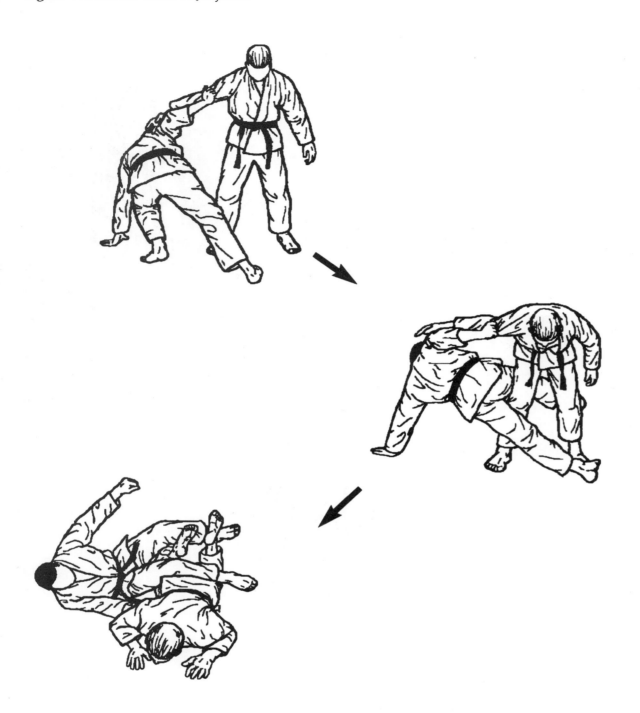

Hasame-gaeshi front

Start in formal position. Reach over the top of his right elbow and grab it with your right hand. Step forward with your left leg bend deeply and duck under his extended right hand. Place your left palm onto the ground and place your right leg behind his legs. Jump backwards and scissors the adversary's legs by hitting the back of his knees with your right leg and the front of his legs at the bottom of his shins with your left leg. The adversary will fall to his face.

Hasame-gaeshi rear

Start in formal position. Pivot 180 degrees on your left leg while maintaining control of the adversary's elbow with your left hand. Place your right palm on the ground. Jump forward and scissors the adversary, striking him at the waist with your left leg and just above his left sole with your right leg. He will be thrown to his back.

Ushiro-guruma

Start in formal position. Step diagonally across with your right foot. Pull the adversary's right arm at his elbow. Lift up on his right elbow by turning the knife edge of your right hand towards the sky. Attempt to headlock the adversary. The adversary will lower his center of gravity and push up on your right hand. He will then execute a rear body grab below the arms. Step in with your left foot so that both feet are between his legs. Clamp down on him with your biceps pulling him in tight. Bend forward at the waist draping the adversary onto your back. Bend your left knee and bring your left heel to your right hip. Look to the left and turn your shoulders to the left throwing the adversary over your right side.

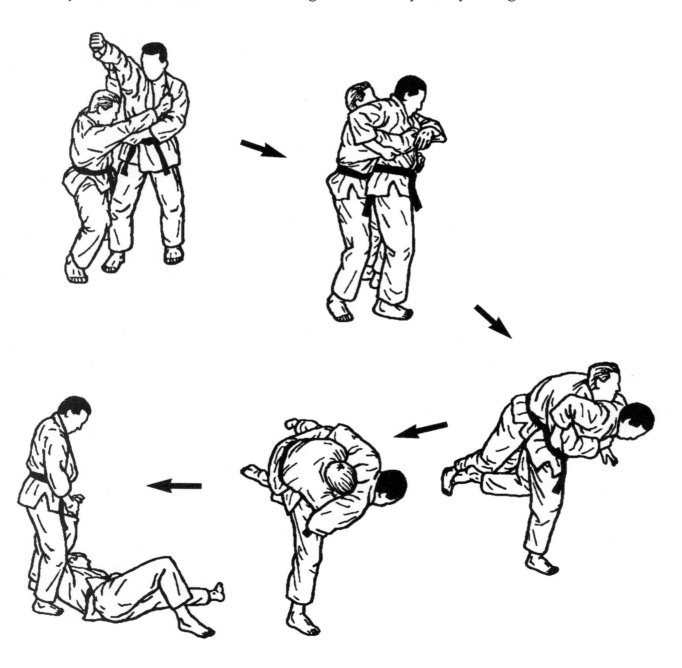

Ground Controls

Uke on back 1

The adversary lies on his back. Grab his right wrist with your left hand. Place your right hand against his throat. Kneel with your right knee on his solar plexus. Brace his right elbow across your knee applying pressure in the direction of the knife edge of his hand until he submits.

Uke on back 2

Adversary lies on his back. Straddle the adversary, sitting on his abdomen and bring your knees in tight. Grab his right wrist with your left hand and grab his throat with your right hand applying Koko. Turn his wrist so that the knife edge of his hand is facing toward you. Brace his elbow against your left thigh.

Uke on back 3

Kneel beside the right side of the adversary who is lying on his back. Reach in underneath the adversary's right elbow with your right hand and grab his right hand with your fingers placed on the back of hand. Place your right knee on the adversary's chest. Pull his wrist towards you. Apply pressure against his shoulder and wrist until he submits.

Uke on back 4

Grab the adversary's right wrists with both hands as he lies on his back. Pull his hand up towards your chest. Step over his head with your left leg and fall to your back. Press your knees tightly together. The knife edge of his hand should be placed against your chest. Apply pressure against his elbow until he submits.

Uke on stomach 1

Stand to the right side of the adversary who is lying on his back. Grab the adversary's right wrist with your left hand. Place your right hand on his elbow and turn him to his front as you step forward with your left leg. Step forward and immobilize the adversary as you place your right knee against his elbow.

Uke on stomach 2

Stand to the right side of the adversary. Kneel on his shoulder blade with your left knee. Immobilize the adversary by pinning his elbow between your knees and levering his arm across his head until he submits. Continue to apply pressure on his wrist pressing it towards his head until he submits.

Uke on stomach 3

Stand to the right side of the adversary. Immobilize the adversary by pinning his elbow between your knees and placing your left knee on his shoulder. Grab his wrist with your right hand as if you were shaking his hand. Apply pressure on his wrist twisting it in towards the knife edge of the hand until he submits.

Uke on stomach 4

The adversary lies on his front. Extend the adversary's left arm. Grab his left wrist with your left hand and press down on his shoulder with your right hand. Drive your knee against the adversary's elbow. The knife edge of his hand should be toward you.

Uke on stomach 5

Kneel at the left side of the adversary who is lying face down. Grab his left arm at the wrist with your left hand and twist it behind his back. Hook your left hand around his wrist and pull his wrist toward you. Press down on his shoulder with your right hand to control the adversary. Continue to apply pressure until he submits.

Uke on stomach 6

Kneel at the left side of the adversary who is lying face down. Grab his left arm at the wrist with your right hand and twist it behind his back. Hook your arm around his wrist and pull his wrist toward you. Press down on his shoulder with your left hand to control the adversary. Continue to apply pressure until he submits.

Uke on stomach 7

The adversary lies in a prostrate position. Grab his right wrist with both hands and extend his hand. The knife edge of his hand should be pointing upwards. Sit through with your left leg and apply pressure to his elbow with your armpit until he submits.

Uke on side 1

Kneel at the adversary's right side as he lies on his back. Suddenly the adversary throws a left roundhouse punch at your head. Slip the punch by moving your head to the left. Cup his left elbow with both hands. Trap his left wrist against the right side of your neck. Turn his elbow so that the knife edge of his hand is facing upward. Apply pressure to his elbow by pulling down and toward your body until he submits.

Tai-sabaki

Tai-sabaki escape and punishment 1

Stand in a natural position facing adversary. Step forward into a right front stance. Inhale sharply and execute a right circular block against the adversary's hooking left punch. Block the arm before it passes the shoulder. Keep your chest forward and your weight should be towards the ball of your feet. Cock your left hand, making a tight fist. Twist your hips forward and execute a Seiken strike to the adversary's jaw.

Tai-sabaki escape and punishment 2

Stand in a natural position facing adversary. Step forward into a left front stance. Inhale sharply and execute a left circular block against the adversary's hooking right punch. Block the arm before it passes the shoulder. Keep your chest forward and your weight should be towards the ball of your feet. Cock your right hand, making a tight fist. Twist your hips forward and execute a Seiken punch to his jaw.

Tai-sabaki escape and punishment 3

Stand in a natural position facing adversary. Avoid the adversary's left straight punch to the head by stepping laterally to the right and slightly forward, dropping your center of gravity. Parry with your left hand. Execute a Seiken strike to the adversary's kidney.

Tai-sabaki escape and punishment 4

Stand in a natural position facing adversary. Avoid the adversary's right straight punch to the head by stepping laterally to the left and slightly forward, dropping your center of gravity. Parry with the right hand. Execute a Seiken strike to the adversary's kidney.

Pg 90 Advanced Combat Ju-jutsu

Tai-sabaki escape and punishment 5

Stand in a natural position facing adversary. As the adversary attacks with a left straight punch to your stomach. Step forward with your right foot and pivot 180 degrees counterclockwise with your buttocks against his. Bring your left hand up and over the adversary's attacking arm. Grab his arm at the wrist. Pull his elbow against your upper ribs at breast level bringing him forward. Before he can regain his balance apply Kote-gaeshi #3. Step around the adversary rotating his hand toward the knife edge. Apply ground control Uke on stomach 2.

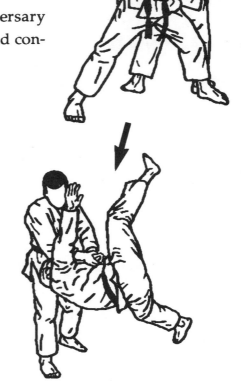

Tai-sabaki escape and punishment 6

Stand in a natural position facing adversary. As the adversary attacks with a right straight punch to your stomach. Step forward with your left foot and pivot 180 degrees clockwise with your buttocks against his buttocks. Bring your left hand up and over the adversary's attacking arm. Grab his arm at the wrist. Pull the man against your upper ribs at breast level bringing him forward. Before he can regain his balance apply Kote-gaeshi #3. Step around the adversary rotating his hand toward the knife edge. Apply ground control Uke on stomach 2.

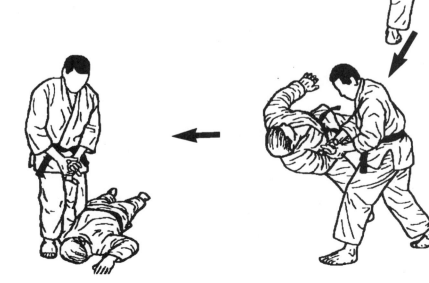

Tai-sabaki escape and punishment 7

Stand in a natural position facing adversary. Inhale sharply and execute a left circular block against the adversary's looping right punch as you step back with your right foot. Keep your chest forward and your weight should be towards the ball of your feet. Cock your right hand, making a tight fist. Twist your hips forward and strike to the adversary's jaw with Seiken.

Tai-sabaki escape and punishment 8

Stand in a natural position facing adversary. Inhale sharply and execute a right circular block against the adversary's looping left punch and step back with your left foot. Keep your chest forward and your weight should be towards the ball of your feet. Cock your left hand, making a tight fist. Twist your hips forward and execute a Seiken strike towards the adversary's jaw.

Tai-sabaki escape and punishment 9

Stand in a natural position facing adversary. As the adversary attacks with a rushing right push wait until the last possible moment to move. Pivot on the ball of your right foot and step back with your left leg avoiding the push. Grab the adversary's extended arm. While turning counter clockwise and drop to your right knee, pulling the adversary's arm outward. Continue to pull the adversary's arm between his legs, forming a full circle. Strike Shuto to the adversary's jaw. Use a downward chopping motion. Note that he is thrown by his own force, your pulling action redirects his momentum.

Tai-sabaki escape and punishment 10

Stand in a natural position facing adversary. As the adversary attacks with a rushing left push wait until the last possible moment to move. Pivot on the ball of your left foot and step back with the right leg to avoid the push. Grab the adversary's extended arm. While turning clockwise drop to your left knee, pulling the adversary's arm outward. Continue to pull the adversary's arm between his legs, forming a full circle. Strike to the adversary's jaw. Note that he is thrown by his own force, your pulling action redirects his momentum.

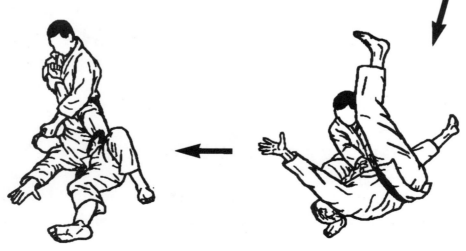

Tai-sabaki Uraken 1

Stand in a natural position facing adversary. As the adversary attacks with a looping left roundhouse punch, step forward into a right front stance. Inhale sharply and execute a right circular block to his forearm. Keep your chest forward and your weight should be towards the ball of your feet. Cock your left hand, making a tight fist. Execute a snapping right Uraken to his nose.

Tai-sabaki Uraken 2

Stand in a natural position facing adversary. As the adversary attacks with a looping right roundhouse punch, step forward into a left front stance. Inhale sharply and execute a left circular block to his forearm. Keep your chest forward and your weight should be towards the ball of your feet. Cock your right hand, making a tight fist. Execute a snapping left Uraken to his nose.

Tai-sabaki Uraken 3

Stand in a natural position facing adversary. As the adversary attacks with a left straight punch to your face. Step laterally to the right and slightly forward, dropping your center of gravity. Parry with the left hand against his extended left wrist. Grab his arm with your left hand, break his elbow across your chest and execute a snapping right back-fist to his nose.

Tai-sabaki Uraken 4

Stand in a natural position facing adversary. As the adversary attacks with a right straight punch to your face. Step laterally to the left and slightly forward, dropping your center of gravity. Parry with the right hand against his extended right forearm. Grab his arm with your right hand, break his elbow across your chest and execute a snapping left back-fist to his nose.

Tai-sabaki Uraken 5

Stand in a natural position facing adversary. As the adversary attacks with a left straight punch to your stomach. Take a token step forward with your right leg. Pivot 180 degrees counterclockwise on your right foot. Strike his extended left wrist with your right forearm. Execute a snapping right back-fist to his nose. Go directly from his wrist to his nose.

Tai-sabaki Uraken 6

Stand in a natural position facing adversary. As the adversary attacks with a right straight punch to your stomach. Take a token step forward with your left leg. Pivot 180 degrees clockwise on your left foot. Strike his extended right wrist with your left forearm. Execute a snapping left back-fist to his nose. Go directly from his wrist to his nose.

Tai-sabaki Uraken 7

Stand in a natural position facing adversary. As the adversary attacks with a hard driving, wild looping right roundhouse punch, step back with your right foot into a left front stance. Tai-sabaki 2 is impractical because of the force of the attack. Inhale sharply and execute a left circular block to his forearm. Keep your chest forward and your weight should be towards the ball of your feet. Cock your right hand, making a tight fist. Twist your hips forward. Execute a snapping left back-fist to his nose.

Tai-sabaki Uraken 8

Stand in a natural position facing adversary. As the adversary attacks with a hard driving, wild looping left roundhouse punch, step back with your left foot into a right front stance. Tai-sabaki 1 is impractical because of the force of the attack. Inhale sharply and execute a right circular block to his forearm. Keep your chest forward and your weight should be towards the ball of your feet. Cock your left hand, making a tight fist. Twist your hips forward. Execute a snapping right back-fist to his nose.

Tai-sabaki Uraken 9

Stand in a natural position facing adversary. As the adversary attacks with a rushing right push wait until the last possible moment to move. Pivot on the ball of your right foot and step back with your right leg avoiding the push. Parry the adversary's wrist with your right hand. Execute a snapping right back-fist to the adversary's nose.

Tai-sabaki Uraken 10

Stand in a natural position facing adversary. As the adversary attacks with a rushing left push wait until the last possible moment to move. Pivot on the ball of your left foot and step back on your right leg avoiding the push. Parry the adversary's wrist with your left hand. Execute a snapping left back-fist to the adversary's nose.

Tai-sabaki cat step 1

Stand in a natural position facing adversary. As the adversary attacks with a looping left roundhouse punch, step forward slightly with your right foot and bob and weave below the adversary's swinging punch. Keep your back straight.

Tai-sabaki cat step 2

Stand in a natural position facing adversary. As the adversary attacks with a looping right roundhouse punch, step forward slightly with your left foot and bob and weave below the adversary's swinging punch. Keep your back straight.

Tai-sabaki cat step 3

Stand in a natural position facing adversary. As the adversary attacks with a left straight punch to your face. Step laterally to the right and slightly forward, dropping your center of gravity. Avoid the punch completely.

Tai-sabaki cat step 4

Stand in a natural position facing adversary. As the adversary attacks with a right straight punch to your face. Step laterally to the left and slightly forward, dropping your center of gravity. Avoid the punch completely.

Tai-sabaki cat step 5

Stand in a natural position facing adversary. As the adversary attacks with a left straight punch to your stomach take a token step forward with your right foot. Pivot 180 degrees counter clockwise on your right foot.

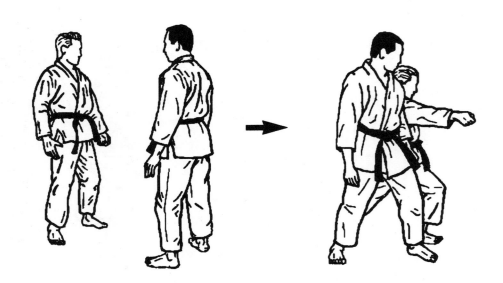

Tai-sabaki cat step 6

Stand in a natural position facing adversary. As the adversary attacks with a right straight punch to your stomach take a token step forward with your left leg. Pivot 180 degrees clockwise on your left foot.

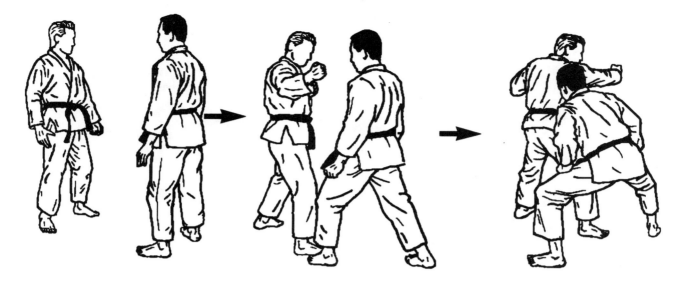

Tai-sabaki cat step 7

Stand in a natural position facing adversary. As the adversary attacks with a hard driving, wild looping right roundhouse punch, step back with your right foot into a left front stance. Bob and weave and avoid the punch completely.

Tai-sabaki cat step 8

Stand in a natural position facing adversary. As the adversary attacks with a hard driving, wild looping left roundhouse punch, step back with your left foot into a right front stance. Bob and weave and avoid the punch completely.

Tai-sabaki cat step 9

Stand in a natural position facing adversary. As the adversary attacks with a rushing right push wait until the last possible moment to move. Pivot 90 degrees on your right foot counter clockwise, step back with your left leg and avoid the push.

Tai-sabaki cat step 10

Stand in a natural position facing adversary. As the adversary attacks with a rushing left push wait until the last possible moment to move. Pivot on the ball of your left foot 90 degrees clockwise step back with your right leg and avoid the push.

Tai-sabaki kicking 1

Stand in a natural position facing adversary. As the adversary attacks with a looping left roundhouse punch, step forward into a right front stance. Inhale sharply and execute a right circular block. Keep your chest forward and your weight should be towards the balls of your feet. Grab his wrist. Cock your left hand, making a tight fist. Twist your hips forward and strike right Mae-geri.

Tai-sabaki kicking 2

Stand in a natural position facing adversary. As the adversary attacks with a looping right roundhouse punch, step forward into a left front stance. Inhale sharply and execute a left circular block. Keep your chest forward and your weight should be towards the balls of your feet. Grab his wrist. Cock your right hand, making a tight fist. Twist your hips forward and strike left Mae-geri.

Tai-sabaki kicking 3

Stand in a natural position facing adversary. As the adversary attacks with a left straight punch to your face. Step laterally to the right and slightly forward, dropping your center of gravity. Parry with the left hand against his extended left wrist. Grab his wrist. Strike with left Mawashi-geri to his solar plexus.

Tai-sabaki kicking 4

Stand in a natural position facing adversary. As the adversary attacks with a right straight punch to your face. Step laterally to the left and slightly forward, dropping your center of gravity. Parry with the right hand against his extended right wrist. Grab his arm. Strike with right Mawashi-geri to his solar plexus.

Tai-sabaki kicking 5

Stand in a natural position facing adversary. As the adversary attacks with a left straight punch to your stomach step forward and wipe his extended arm away with your right hand. Grab his wrist. Take a token step forward with your right foot. Pivot 180 degrees on your right foot and strike with a right Yoko-geri to his lower rib cage.

Tai-sabaki kicking 6

Stand in a natural position facing adversary. As the adversary attacks with a right straight punch to your stomach Take a token step forward with your right foot, wipe his extended arm away with your left hand. Grab his wrist. Pivot 180 degrees on your left foot and strike with a left Yoko-geri to his lower rib cage.

Tai-sabaki kicking 7

Stand in a natural position facing adversary. As the adversary attacks with a hard driving, wild looping right roundhouse punch, step back with your right foot into a left front stance. Tai-sabaki 2 is impractical because of the force of the attack. Inhale sharply and execute a left circular block. Keep your chest forward and your weight should be towards the ball of your feet. Cock your right hand, making a tight fist. Twist your hips forward. Strike to the adversary's stomach with a left Mae-geri.

Tai-sabaki kicking 8

Stand in a natural position facing adversary. As the adversary attacks with a hard driving, wild looping left roundhouse punch, step back with your left foot into a right front stance. Tai-sabaki 1 is impractical because of the force of the attack. Inhale sharply and execute a right circular block. Keep your chest forward and your weight should be towards the ball of your feet. Cock your left hand, making a tight fist. Twist your hips forward. Strike to the adversary's stomach with a right Mae-geri.

Tai-sabaki kicking 9

Stand in a natural position facing adversary. As the adversary attacks with a rushing right push wait until the last possible moment to move. Pivot 90 degrees counter clockwise on your right foot, step back with your left leg and avoid the push. Strike with a right Yoko-geri to the adversary's lower rib cage.

Tai-sabaki kicking 10

Stand in a natural position facing adversary. As the adversary attacks with a rushing left push wait until the last possible moment to move. Pivot 90 degrees clockwise on the ball of your left foot step back with the left leg and avoid the push. Strike with a left Yoko-geri to the adversary's lower rib cage.

Tai-sabaki with throws 1

Stand in a natural position facing adversary. As the adversary attacks with a looping left roundhouse punch, step forward into a right front stance. Lower your center of gravity. Inhale sharply and execute a right circular block. Keep your chest forward and your weight should be towards the ball of your feet. Cock your left hand, making a tight fist. Twist your hips forward. Strike with a left forearm to the adversary's neck and throw him to his back with left Koshi-guruma. Finish with a Seiken to his jaw.

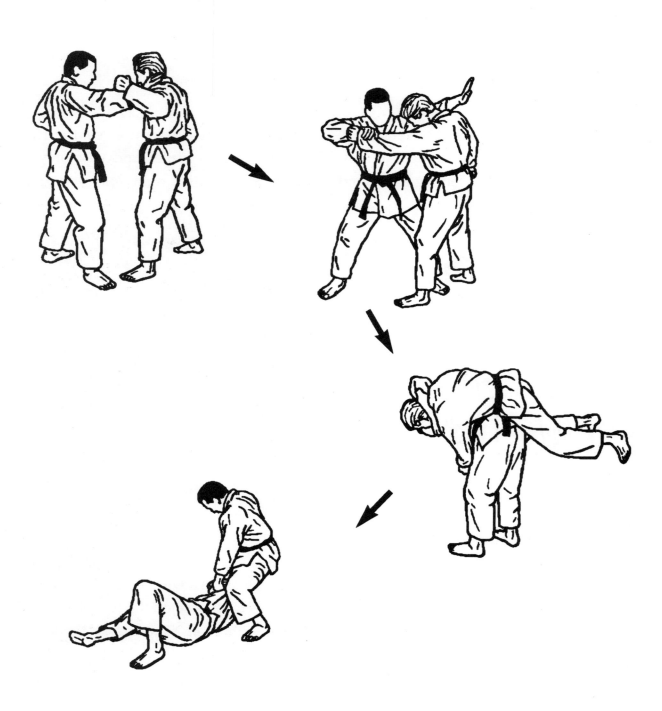

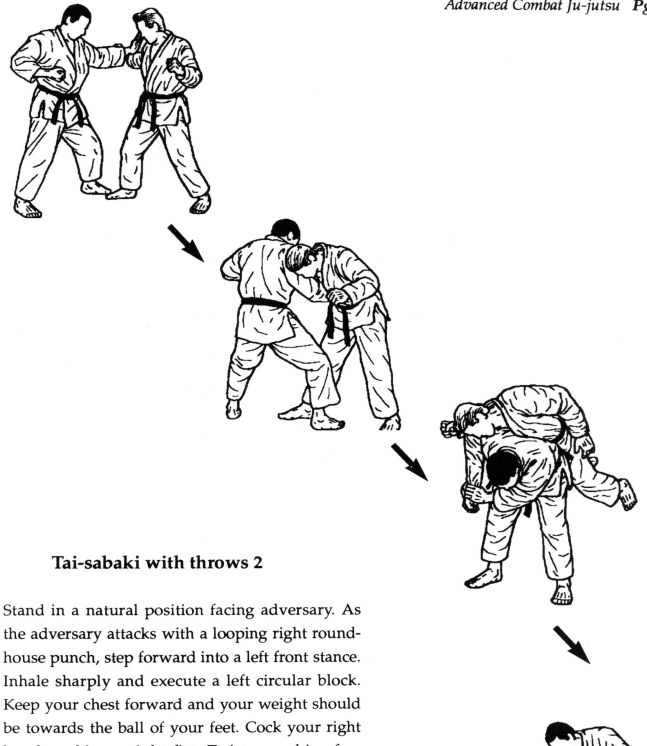

Tai-sabaki with throws 2

Stand in a natural position facing adversary. As the adversary attacks with a looping right roundhouse punch, step forward into a left front stance. Inhale sharply and execute a left circular block. Keep your chest forward and your weight should be towards the ball of your feet. Cock your right hand, making a tight fist. Twist your hips forward. Strike with a glancing right empi to the adversary's lower rib cage. Execute Ippon seio nage and throw the adversary to his back. Finish with a Seiken to his jaw.

Pg 112 Advanced Combat Ju-jutsu

Tai-sabaki with throws 3

Stand in a natural position facing the adversary. As the adversary attacks with a left straight punch to your face. Step laterally to the right and slightly forward, dropping your center of gravity. Cross block with the right hand against his extended left wrist. Grab his hand with your right hand and place it on your neck and simultaneously strike to the bend in the adversary's right elbow with a left forearm off-balancing him. Throw him with right sided Osoto-gari reaping his left leg. Finish with a right Seiken to his jaw.

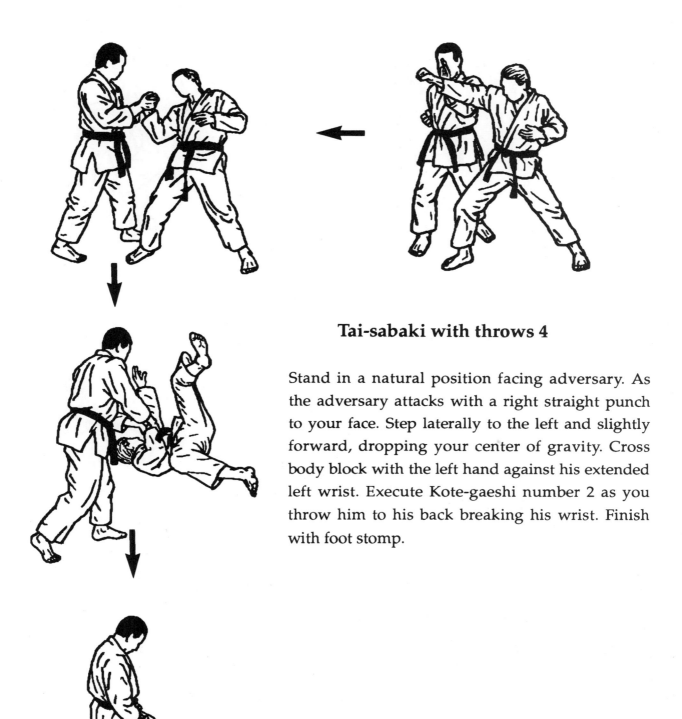

Tai-sabaki with throws 4

Stand in a natural position facing adversary. As the adversary attacks with a right straight punch to your face. Step laterally to the left and slightly forward, dropping your center of gravity. Cross body block with the left hand against his extended left wrist. Execute Kote-gaeshi number 2 as you throw him to his back breaking his wrist. Finish with foot stomp.

Pg 114 Advanced Combat Ju-jutsu

Tai-sabaki with throws 5

Stand in a natural position facing adversary. As the adversary attacks with a left straight punch to your stomach. Step forward with your right foot and pivot 180 degrees Counter clockwise so that your buttocks touch his buttocks. Bring your left hand up and over the adversary's attacking arm. Grab his arm at the wrist. Pull the man against your upper ribs at breast level bringing him forward. Before he can regain his balance apply Kote-gaeshi #3. Step around the adversary rotating his hand toward the knife edge. Apply ground control Uke on stomach 2.

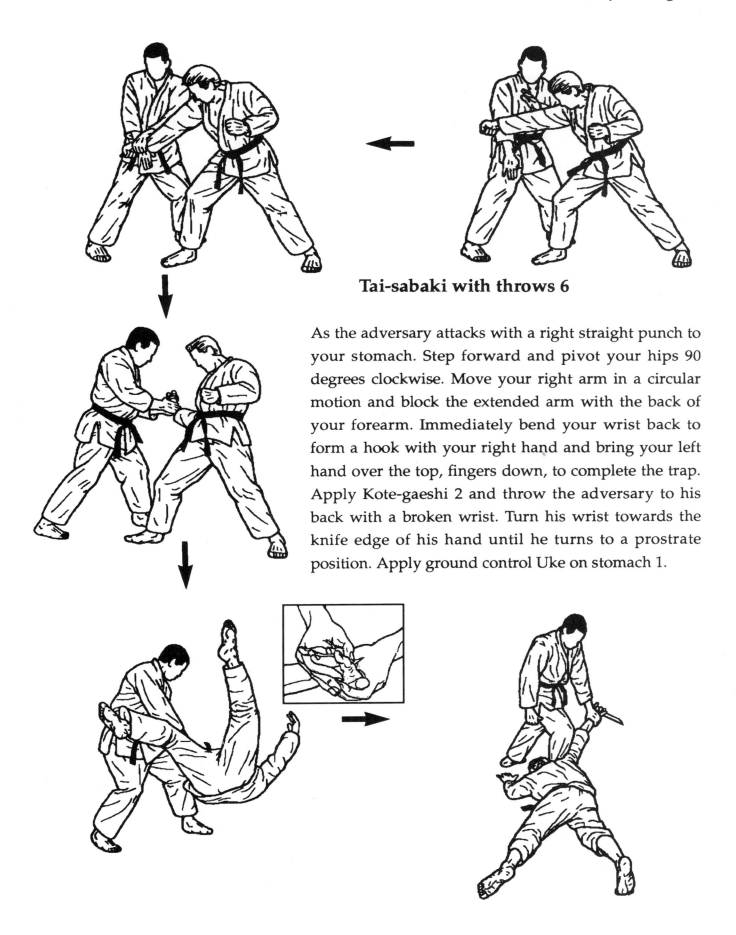

Tai-sabaki with throws 6

As the adversary attacks with a right straight punch to your stomach. Step forward and pivot your hips 90 degrees clockwise. Move your right arm in a circular motion and block the extended arm with the back of your forearm. Immediately bend your wrist back to form a hook with your right hand and bring your left hand over the top, fingers down, to complete the trap. Apply Kote-gaeshi 2 and throw the adversary to his back with a broken wrist. Turn his wrist towards the knife edge of his hand until he turns to a prostrate position. Apply ground control Uke on stomach 1.

Tai-sabaki with throws 7

Stand in a natural position facing adversary. As the adversary attacks with a hard driving, wild looping right roundhouse punch, step back with your right foot into a left front stance. Tai-sabaki 2 is impractical because of the force of the attack. Inhale sharply and execute a left circular block. Keep your chest forward and your weight should be towards the ball of your feet. Cock your right hand, making a tight fist. Twist your hips forward. Strike with a right forearm to the adversary's neck and execute Harai-goshi. Finish with a stomp to the adversary's head.

Tai sabaki with throws 8

Stand in a natural position facing adversary. As the adversary attacks with a hard driving, wild looping left roundhouse punch, step back with your left foot into a right front stance. Tai-sabaki 1 is impractical because of the force of the attack. Inhale sharply and execute a right circular block. Keep your chest forward and your weight should be towards the ball of your feet. Cock your left hand, making a tight fist. Twist your hips forward. Strike with a left forearm to the adversary's rib cage and execute Ogoshi. Finish with a Seiken to the adversary's head.

Tai-sabaki with throws 9

Stand in a natural position facing adversary. As the adversary attacks with a rushing right push wait until the last possible moment to move. Pivot on the ball of your right foot 90 degrees counter clockwise and step back with the left foot avoiding the push. Grab the adversary's extended arm and execute Judo Tai-otoshi. Strike Seiken to the adversary's jaw. Note that he is thrown by his own force, your pulling action redirects his momentum.

Tai-sabaki with throws 10

Stand in a natural position facing adversary. As the adversary attacks with a rushing left push wait until the last possible moment to move. Pivot on the ball of your left foot 90 degrees clockwise and step back with your right leg to avoid the push. Grab the adversary's extended arm. Execute Uki-otoshi. Strike to the adversary's jaw. Note that he is thrown by his own force, your pulling action redirects his momentum.

Strategy

To successfully defend himself, the warrior was able to quickly analyze the assault, prepare a plan of action with alternatives and, immediately gain control of the situation. Combat Ju-jutsu practitioners are taught strategy by lecture as well as through various self-defense drills that simulate assaults as they might actually occur on the streets. There are four stages of strategy that allow you to accomplish your objectives. They are assessing the potential threat, using your environment, adjusting your focus, and utilizing a complete attack.

In a violent confrontation you can count on attacks from more than one adversary. You must attempt to identify potential adversaries and accomplices. Sometimes potential adversaries are obvious; for example, you are involved in a car accident and two adversaries jump out of the automobile and attempt to assault you. At other times, an accomplice may be hiding behind a doorway.

In addition to identifying the adversaries, you must identify other potential threats. How is the adversary holding his hands? Does it look like he is carrying a concealed weapon? These are the types of questions that may save your life. Miyama Ryu Ju-jutsu training provides solutions to many of these situations. For example, the basic defense techniques against a knife thrust to the stomach involve the defender turning 180 degrees, which allows him to see other potential assailants.

Using your environment is vital to reacting to threats. Identifying potential exits or areas that you can use for cover may allow you to avert danger in many instances. Additionally, the environment provides us with a myriad of weapons ranging from items as innocuous as a ballpoint pen, which can be used to attack vital areas, or a weapon as obvious as a baseball bat. The Miyama Ryu unarmed techniques easily incorporate these environmental weapons. The overriding objective of Combat Ju-jutsu is to survive a violent encounter; so a response such as smashing someone over the head with a chair is as acceptable as using a joint-locking technique.

Although Miyama Ryu Ju-jutsu exponents train in the classical weaponry used by the samurai warriors and modern weapons carried by street thugs, carrying a device used specifically for a weapon is discouraged. In a life-and-death situation you will become psychologically dependent on your weapon. For example, if you have to defend yourself and you are carrying a knife, you will attempt to use this knife, even if it is not your best option. Whereas, if you picked up a chair to strike the adversary and this strategy was thwarted, chances are that you would not worry too much about retrieving it since you only used it because it was convenient.

Strategy

The ability to adjust your focus is an integral part of a successful self-defense strategy. When you engage an adversary, your attention is focused on defeating him. In some circumstances it is necessary to focus on the adversary. For example, if you are attacked with a right stick to the side of the head, you would attack the arm and not the stick.

When you are finished with one adversary you must switch your focus automatically to the others. If you do not adjust quickly, you will develop tunnel vision. During a multiple-man attack, tunnel vision could have fatal consequences. Don't win the battle and lose the war.

The final phase of self-defense strategy is to understand and utilize the complete technique. The complete technique consists of: an evasion or block of the initial attack; a strike to loosen up the adversary and take his focus away from his intended attack; a major technique such as a throw, joint-lock or choke; and a finishing strike or ground control to immobilize the attacker. The ground control is sometimes preceded by a strike if the attacker is still active and you want to control him. In the Miyama Ryu, for multiple-man attacks ground strikes and controls are never employed because you are always looking for your next attacker.

The following techniques show potential responses to violent attacks that you might encounter on the street. They are intended as a guide only as other viable responses may be taken from any of the student's basics. Miyama Ryu is a flexible art that allows a student to be creative, while keeping their defensive reactions realistic and simple.

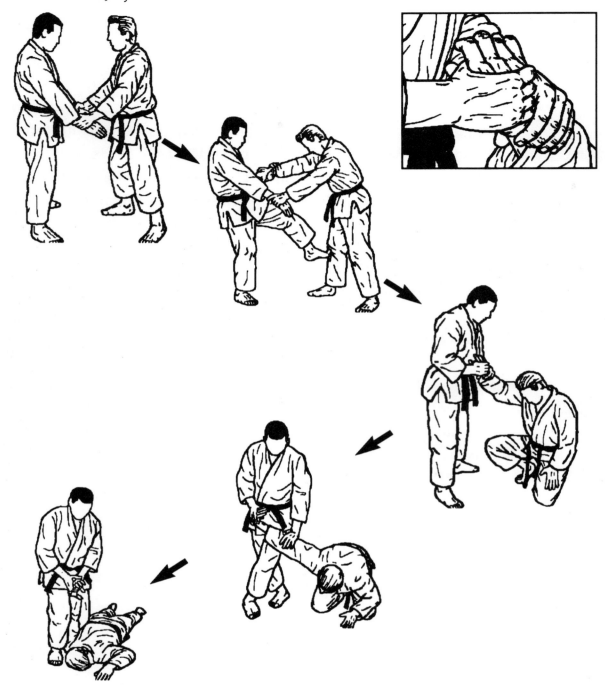

Double wrist grab Nikyo

The adversary grabs both your wrists with his hands. Grab his left wrist upwards as you strike to his knee with a left Mae-geri. Reach over with your right hand. Grab his left hand. Execute a Nikyo breaking his left wrist. Place your left hand on his elbow and force him to the ground. Apply ground control Uke on stomach 2.

Safety considerations: When pressure is felt from the Nikyo, Uke should slap his body repeatedly to signal pain. Uke should slap again on the ground when the ground control is applied.

Single wrist grab Ippon seoi nage

The adversary grabs your left hand with his right hand. Rotate your hand and grab inside his arm at the wrist. Strike with Empi to the adversary's floating rib cage. Throw him to his back with Ippon seoi nage. Apply ground control Uke on back 1.

Safety considerations: Apply the ground control slowly to avoid dislocating the Uke's shoulder.

Pg 124 Advanced Combat Ju-jutsu

Cross wrist grab Devil's handshake

The adversary grabs your right wrist with his right hand. Grab his right wrist. Pull his right hand diagonally across your chest and strike to his face with Uraken. Execute devil's handshake. Extend your left leg, heel up, toes down across his legs. Throw the adversary over your extended leg. Apply ground control Uke on stomach 1.

Safety considerations: Simulate the break by pulling down gradually. Your knee must point down when executing the throw so if the adversary falls on your knee he doesn't dislocate it.

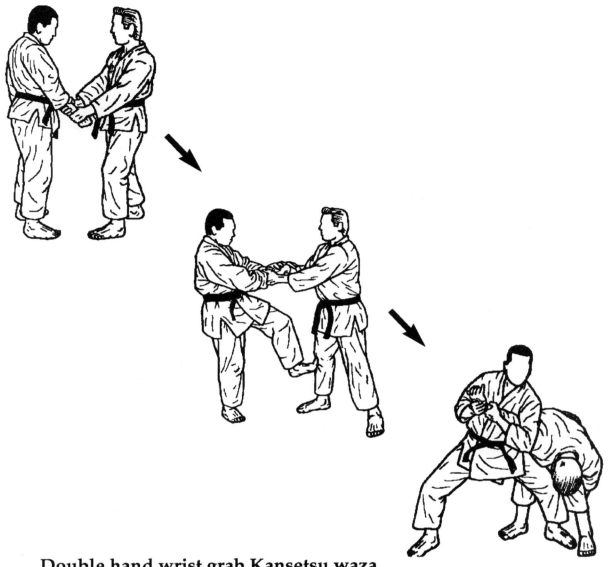

Double hand wrist grab Kansetsu waza

The adversary grabs your right wrist with both hands. Trap his right hand with your left hand and wrap your right hand around his wrist as you execute a left Mae-geri to his knee. Apply Waki-gatame to his elbow and apply ground control Uke on stomach 2.

Safety considerations: The Uke should slap to signal submission.

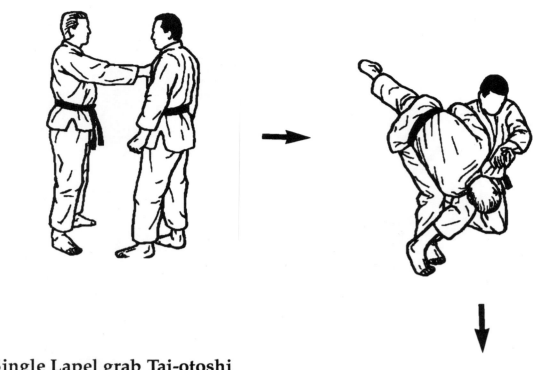

Single Lapel grab Tai-otoshi

The adversary grabs your left lapel with his right hand. Grab his inner wrist with your right hand. Step in with your right leg as you strike with a right Shuto to his jaw. Attack with Ju-jutsu Tai-otoshi. Throw him to his back and finish with a ground strike followed by a ground control.

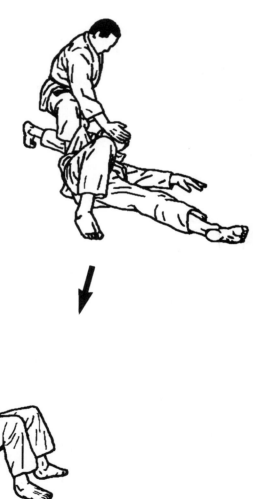

Advanced Combat Ju-jutsu Pg 127

Double Lapel grab Kansetsu waza

The adversary grabs you by both lapels. Reach up with a left handed web grip and grab his right wrist. Strike Seiken to his face with your right hand. Apply Kansetsu waza with wrist pressure.

Safety considerations: The Uke should slap his body to signal submissions.

Cross lapel Kansetsu waza control

The adversary grabs you cross lapel with his right hand to your right lapel. Step forward with your left leg trap his hand to your body with your right hand. Strike left backhand Shuto to the adversary's throat. Reach underneath his elbow with your left hand and grab your right wrist. Break his elbow with a Kansetsu waza control.

Safety considerations: Simulate the break by applying pressure gradually. The Uke should slap his body to signal submission.

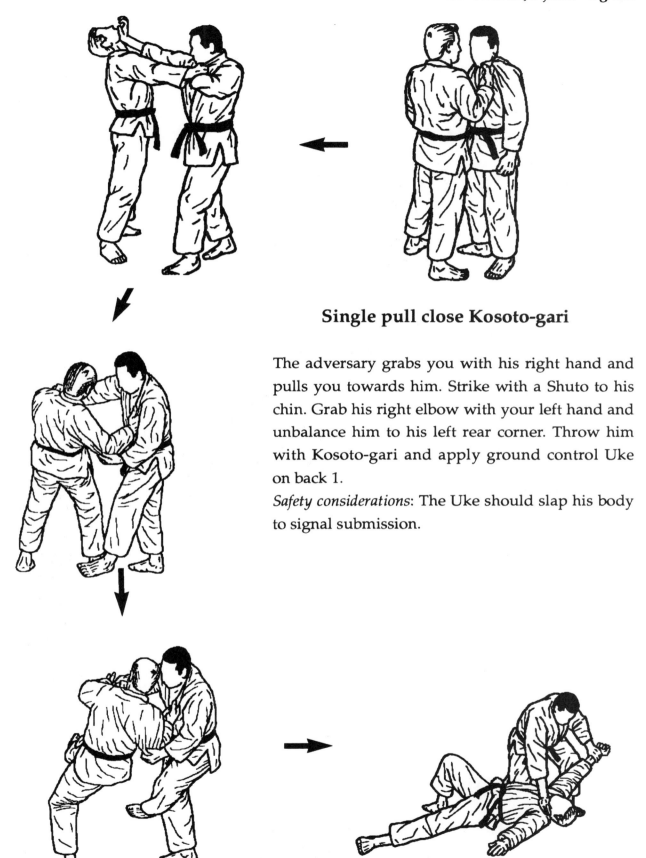

Single pull close Kosoto-gari

The adversary grabs you with his right hand and pulls you towards him. Strike with a Shuto to his chin. Grab his right elbow with your left hand and unbalance him to his left rear corner. Throw him with Kosoto-gari and apply ground control Uke on back 1.

Safety considerations: The Uke should slap his body to signal submission.

Double pull close Harai-goshi

The adversary grabs you with both hands and pulls you towards him. Strike with double Shotei to his ear. Wrap your right hand around his neck and grab his upper arm. Throw him with right sided Harai-goshi to his back. Finish with a stomp to his head.

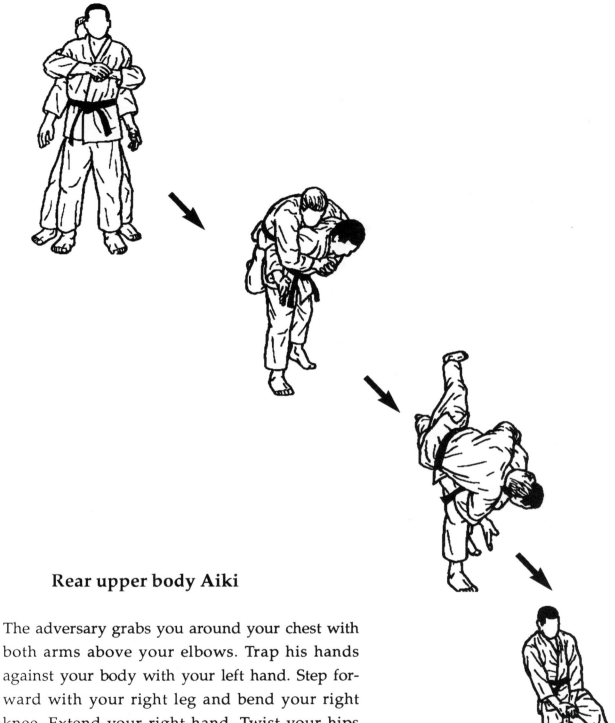

Rear upper body Aiki

The adversary grabs you around your chest with both arms above your elbows. Trap his hands against your body with your left hand. Step forward with your right leg and bend your right knee. Extend your right hand. Twist your hips and throw him across your back to the fall. Follow with a foot stomp to the head.

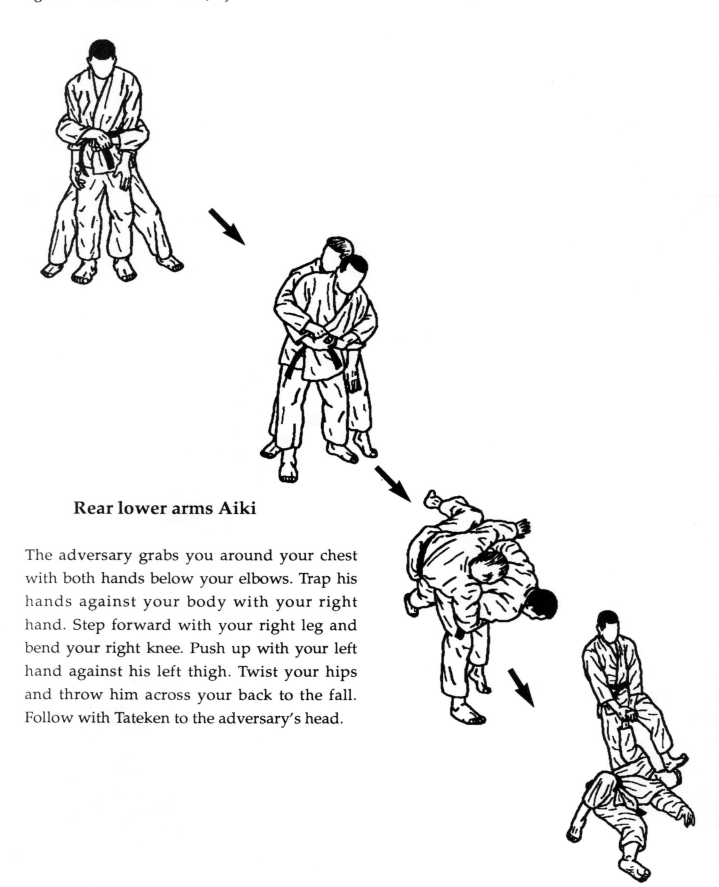

Rear lower arms Aiki

The adversary grabs you around your chest with both hands below your elbows. Trap his hands against your body with your right hand. Step forward with your right leg and bend your right knee. Push up with your left hand against his left thigh. Twist your hips and throw him across your back to the fall. Follow with Tateken to the adversary's head.

Front neck embrace O goshi

The adversary grabs you around the neck with both hands. Lower your weight by bending at the knees. Strike double Shuto to the adversary's ribs. Place your right hand around his waist and your left hand at his upper arm. Throw him to his back with Ogoshi. Finish him with a joint lock.

Safety considerations: The Uke must slap to indicate submission.

Front chest grab under arms Harai-goshi

The adversary grabs you around the chest and under your arms with both hands. Lower your weight by bending at the knees. Strike with both palms to the adversary's ears. Place your right hand around his neck making a fist, and your left hand at his upper arm. Throw him to his back with Harai-goshi reaping below his right knee. Finish him with a punch to his face.

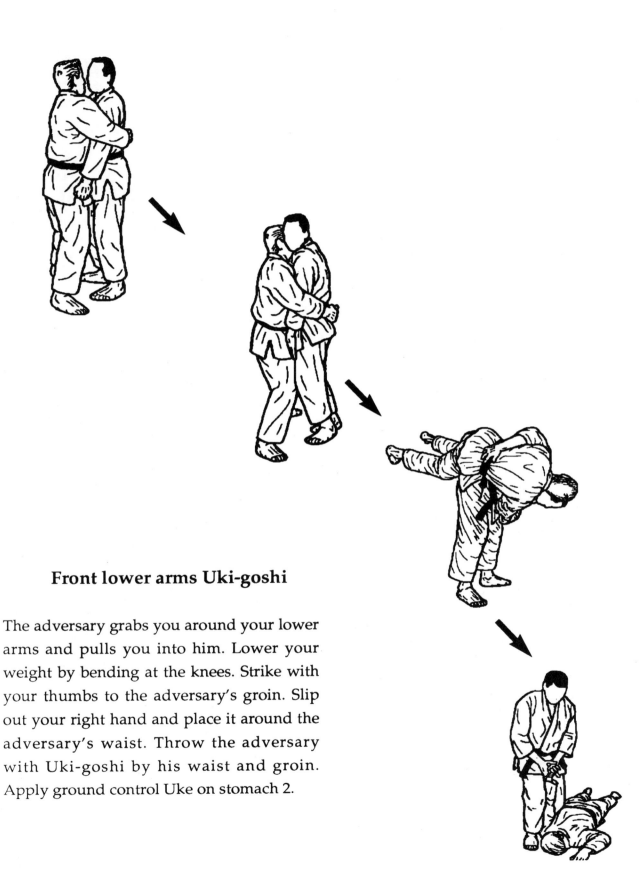

Front lower arms Uki-goshi

The adversary grabs you around your lower arms and pulls you into him. Lower your weight by bending at the knees. Strike with your thumbs to the adversary's groin. Slip out your right hand and place it around the adversary's waist. Throw the adversary with Uki-goshi by his waist and groin. Apply ground control Uke on stomach 2.

Tackle Sumi-gaeshi

The adversary attempts to reap you off your feet by tackling you from the front. Strike with an elbow strike to his spine. Grab his belt, sit between his legs and fall to your back, throwing him over your shoulder.

Safety considerations: Release the Uke so that he takes a roll. Holding onto him could possibly cause his shoulder to become dislocated.

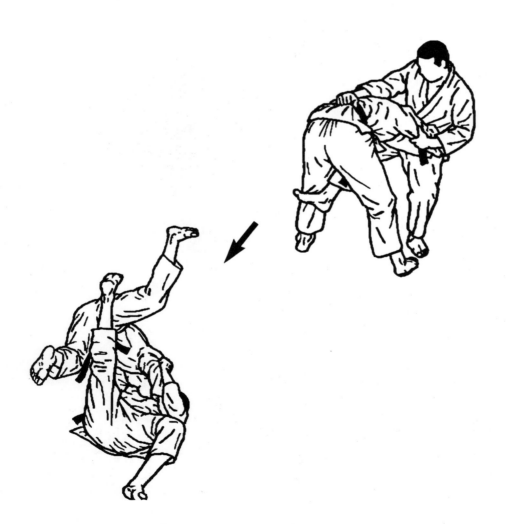

Advanced Combat Ju-jutsu Pg 137

Mug 1

As the adversary seizes you around the throat, turn your head into the bend of his elbow and pull his arm down with your left hand. Simultaneously as you bend your knees strike with Empi with your right elbow to his rib cage. Execute Ippon Seoi nage and throw the adversary to his side. Strike him to the temple with a foot stomp.

Mug 2 (Around the neck unbalance)

The adversary seizes you around the throat and pulls you backwards so that your weight is on your heels. Turn your head into the bend of his arm and pull down on his right arm. Draw a semi-circle back with your right foot to trap the adversary's right leg and unbalance him. Pivot 180 degrees on your right leg. Step behind the adversary with your left leg causing him to fall.

Safety considerations: Uke should slap the ground to indicate submission.

Mug 3

The adversary seizes you around the throat and pulls you backwards so that you are completely unbalanced. Reach up and grab as high as you can with your right hand. Pivot 180 degrees on your right leg so that your left knee ends up between his legs. Bring your right knee to meet your left knee. Throw the adversary to his back and strike Seiken to his face.

Safety considerations: When you go to a kneeling position, place your left hand on the ground so that the Uke has some room to fall and so your face is not driven into the ground.

Mug 4 (flying mare)

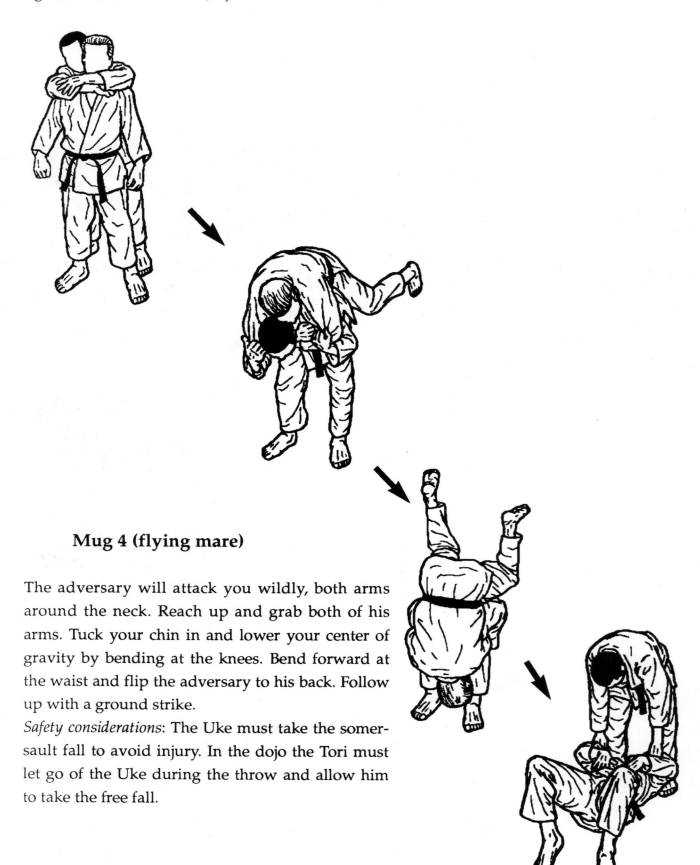

The adversary will attack you wildly, both arms around the neck. Reach up and grab both of his arms. Tuck your chin in and lower your center of gravity by bending at the knees. Bend forward at the waist and flip the adversary to his back. Follow up with a ground strike.

Safety considerations: The Uke must take the somersault fall to avoid injury. In the dojo the Tori must let go of the Uke during the throw and allow him to take the free fall.

Mug 5 (knee in back)

The adversary grabs you around the neck with your right hand and places his knee in the small of your back. Grab above his right elbow with your left hand. Step back with your right leg as you pivot your hips 90 degrees clockwise. Simultaneously bring your right hand down and brush his right knee away from you and towards him. Grab under his thigh with your right hand. Take a token step towards him. Reap his right leg with Osoto-gari and throw him to his back.

Mug 6 (Hand on mouth)

The adversary places his right hand over your mouth and steps back with his left leg pulling you back. Reach up and grab his right hand with your right hand. Step back with your left leg, pivot to your left, extend your right leg heel up, knee down. Throw the adversary with Tai-otoshi over your extended leg.

Mug 7 (Hair pull)

The adversary pulls your head back by the hair. Trap his hand to your head by placing your left hand, then your right over his hand. Step back to the left, pivoting 180 degrees on your right. Apply Sankyo to his wrist. Strike to his lower ribs with Empi and throw him to his back with Ippon seoi nage.

Mug 8 (Ouchi-gari, Kouchi-gari)

Ouchi-gari

The adversary grabs you around the neck and pulls you back on your heels. Reach up with your right hand and grab the adversary's arm above his elbow. Step back 90 degrees and grab the adversary's right calf with your left hand. Pull up on his leg and execute Ouchi gari, reaping his left leg. Strike with a punch to his groin.

Kouchi-gari

The adversary grabs you around the neck and pulls you back on your heels. Reach up with your left hand and grab the adversary's right wrist. Step back 90 degrees and grab the adversary's outer right leg at the knee with your right hand. Pull up on his leg and execute Kouchi gari, sweeping his inner right leg. Strike with a punch to his groin.

Mug 9 (The ouster)

The adversary grabs you by your back collar with his left hand. With his right hand he grabs you by the seat of your pants. He extends his hands and begins to walk you forward. Reach behind you and grab his right elbow. Drop to your right knee. Push up on the elbow and perform Kansetsu waza against the elbow. Bring your right hand forward in a circular manner. Throw the adversary in front of you and to his back.

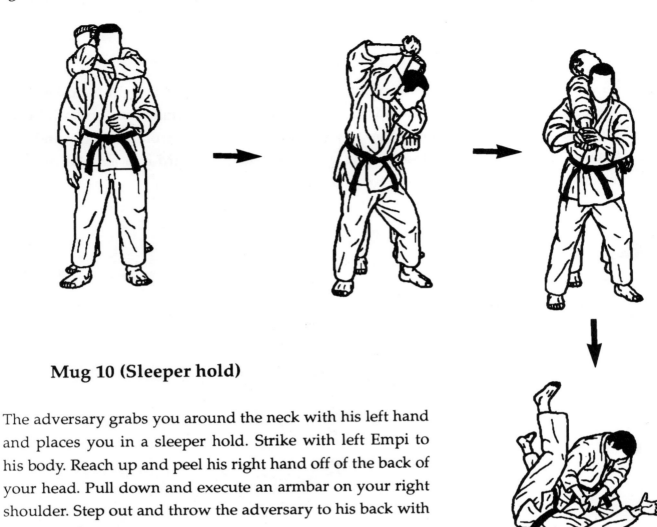

Mug 10 (Sleeper hold)

The adversary grabs you around the neck with his left hand and places you in a sleeper hold. Strike with left Empi to his body. Reach up and peel his right hand off of the back of your head. Pull down and execute an armbar on your right shoulder. Step out and throw the adversary to his back with a Ju-jutsu Seoi nage.

Safety considerations: Simulate the break in class. The Uke must tap the side of his body to indicate submission.

Mug 11 (Walking mug)

The adversary grabs you from behind as you are walking. Drop to your right knee and twist your right shoulder. Grab his right elbow and pull down at the same time which causes the adversary to fall over your back. Strike with Tateken to finish him.

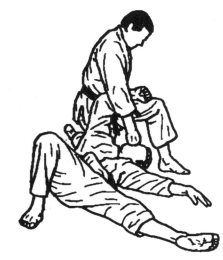

Mug 12 (Full nelson)

The adversary attempts to grab you around the neck with a full nelson. Pull your elbows towards your body loosening the adversary's grip to prevent the full application. Step forward with your right leg and bend your right knee. Twist your hips and throw him across your back to the fall. Push up on his left leg with your right hand. Follow with foot stomp to the head.

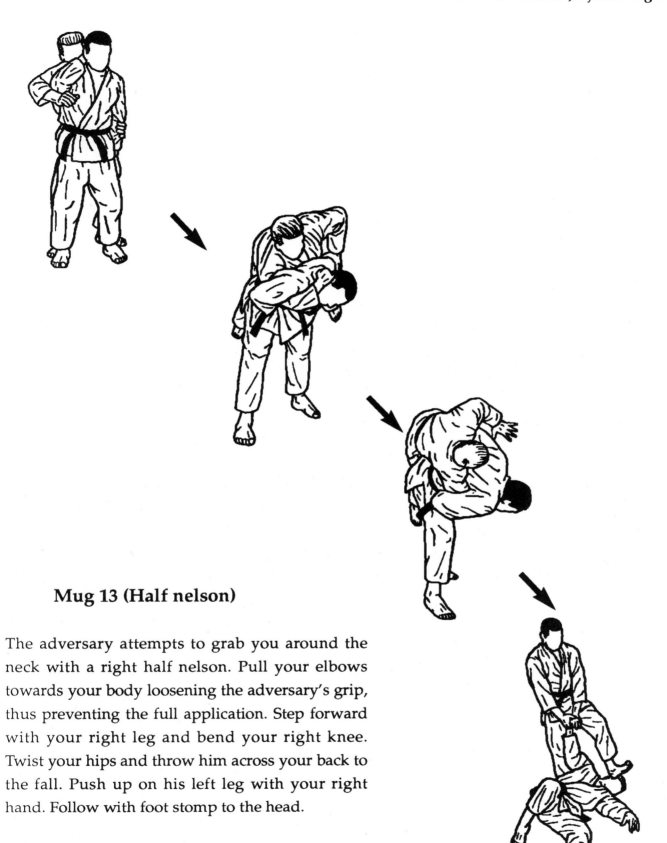

Mug 13 (Half nelson)

The adversary attempts to grab you around the neck with a right half nelson. Pull your elbows towards your body loosening the adversary's grip, thus preventing the full application. Step forward with your right leg and bend your right knee. Twist your hips and throw him across your back to the fall. Push up on his left leg with your right hand. Follow with foot stomp to the head.

Mug 14 (Aiki kneeling)

The adversary grabs you around the neck with his right arm. Step to the side and the rear with your left leg. Reach up with your right hand and grab his right elbow. Drop to your right knee and pull out and then back with your right hand throwing the adversary to the ground.

Mug 15 (Neck grab Goshin Jutsu)

The adversary grabs you around the neck. Grab his right wrist with your left hand and his elbow with your right hand. Pull down sharply. Drive your head under the adversary's armpit. Pivot on your right foot and step back. You should be facing the adversary. The knife edge of his extended hand should face the sky. Bring his elbow perpendicular to the mat. Drive down and break the adversary's elbow. Side step and bring the adversary to his face.

Mug 16 (Hooking)

The adversary grabs you around the neck with his right arm and pulls you back onto your heels. Entangle his right leg with your right leg by wrapping your instep to the outside and around his heel. Pull up and fall directly backwards dislocating his knee.

Safety consideration: Fall to the side and not directly back on the Uke to avoid dislocating the knee.

Mug 17 (Knee dislocation)

The adversary grabs you around the neck with his right arm. Entangle his right leg with your right leg by wrapping your instep to the inside and around his heel. Drive your knee against his knee and throw him to the ground with a dislocated knee.

Front choke Sankyo

The adversary attack with a front choke. Grab with your left hand thumb and fingers up. Strike Empi to his jaw. Strike at the bend in his elbow as you push his right arm up so that his elbow is pointing towards the ceiling. Pivot 180 degrees on your right foot, twisting his wrist with both hands keeping the elbow up. Execute Sankyo and dislocate the adversary's wrist. Step in front of him with your left leg and swing your hands in arc. This action will throw him to the ground.

Rear choke Kansetsu waza

The adversary attacks from the rear with a back choke. Peel his fingers off your neck by grabbing fingers down thumb on the back of his hands. Pull both elbows over your shoulders and fracture them by pulling down. Step diagonally back with your right leg slip under his left arm. Pull his left hand towards you and cross his arms. Drive the crook of his right elbow against his left elbow and throw him to his back.

Safety considerations: Simulate the break in class. The Uke should take a free fall.

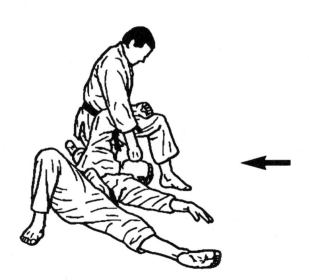

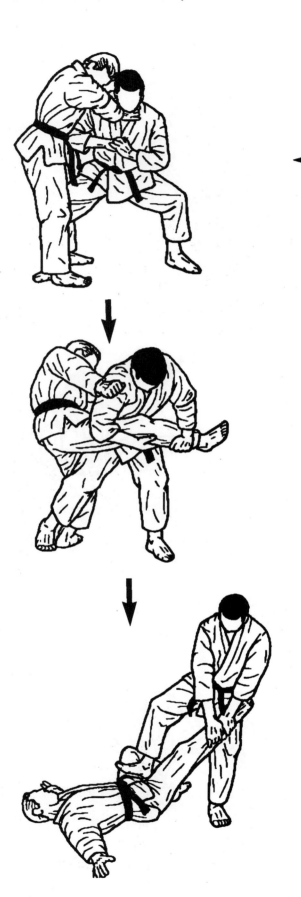

Side choke Ouchi-gari

The adversary attacks at your right side with a double hand choke. Step into a horse stance and strike with your right elbow to his solar plexus. Grab his right leg with both hands and pull up. Execute Ouchi-gari and reap his left leg throwing him to his back. Strike foot stomp to his groin.

Safety considerations: Uke must take a back fall.

Knife carotid stab Kansetsu waza with control

Stand in a natural position. The adversary lunges with an overhead knife stab to your carotid artery. Step forward and turn your hips 90 degrees. Avoid the stab as you extend your right hand out and capture his wrist in the bend of your elbow. Step out with your left leg and go immediately to the ground as you fracture the adversary's elbow with Waki-gatame.
Safety considerations: Do not drive the Uke down too quickly or dislocation will occur.

Knife face cut Tigerlock

Stand in a natural position facing adversary. As the adversary attacks with a knife slash to your face step forward into a left front stance. Inhale sharply and execute a left circular block to his forearm. Keep your chest forward and your weight should be towards the ball of your feet. Execute a right tiger lock. Break the adversary's balance to his right rear corner by pulling him towards your chest. Throw him to his back with Osoto-gari. Continue to maintain pressure on the elbow with the tiger lock.
Safety considerations: Simulate the break in class. The Uke must slap the side of his body to indicate that the Tori has applied sufficient pressure to the lock.

Knife backhand to face Seoi nage

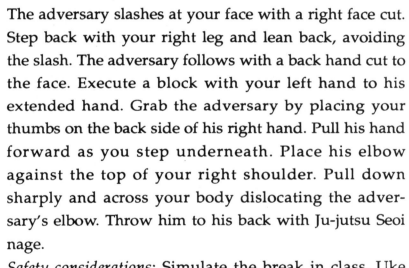

The adversary slashes at your face with a right face cut. Step back with your right leg and lean back, avoiding the slash. The adversary follows with a back hand cut to the face. Execute a block with your left hand to his extended hand. Grab the adversary by placing your thumbs on the back side of his right hand. Pull his hand forward as you step underneath. Place his elbow against the top of your right shoulder. Pull down sharply and across your body dislocating the adversary's elbow. Throw him to his back with Ju-jutsu Seoi nage.

Safety considerations: Simulate the break in class. Uke goes with the technique.

Pg 160   Advanced Combat Ju-jutsu

Knife throat thrust Osoto-gari

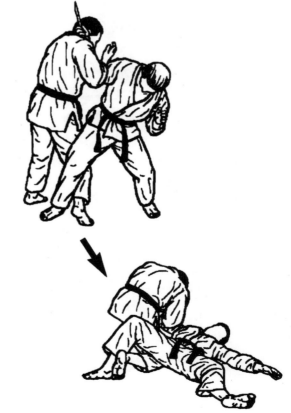

Stand in a natural position facing the adversary. As the adversary attacks with a right straight thrust to your throat. Step forward to the left and turn your body 90 degrees clockwise. Parry with the left hand against his extended right wrist. Grab his hand with your left hand and place it on your neck simultaneously strike to the bend in the adversary's right elbow with a right forearm off balancing him. Throw him with right sided Osoto-gari reaping his right leg and going to a kneeling position so that you are not cut as the adversary is thrown. Finish with a right strike to his jaw.

Knife stomach thrust Haito

The adversary attacks with a right sided thrust to your stomach. Step forward and turn 90 degrees clockwise presenting a smaller target. Slide your left hand, thumb up, under the adversary's wrist and strike to his nose with a right Haito. Execute compound Kote-gaeshi. Stretch him out and apply a ground control.

Knife body slash Yama Arashi

The adversary attacks with a right sided slash to your stomach. Step forward into a right front stance and execute an Empi to the adversary's jaw. Execute a right sided Yama Arashi. The movement from strike to throw should be continuous. Strike the adversary to his face and immobilize the adversary with ground control Uke on back 1.

Safety considerations: The Uke should move his head back to avoid the elbow strike.

Knife back hand body slash Tai-otoshi

The adversary slashes at your face with a right face cut. Step back with your right leg and lean back, avoiding the slash. The adversary follows with a back hand cut to your stomach. Step in and grab the adversary's right wrist with your right hand. Strike the adversary's elbow with the crook of your arm thus fracturing it. Apply a naked devil's handshake. Extend your left leg in front of his legs, heel up, knee down. Throw the adversary with Tai-otoshi.
Safety considerations: Keep your knee pointed towards the ground so that if the adversary falls on it, it will not be dislocated.

Knife disembowlment Kansetsu waza

The adversary attempts to disembowel you with an upwards arcing right stab. Squeeze your fingers together and extend them crossing your wrists, right over left. Block the arcing arm between your wrists as your lower your body into a deep horse stance, forcing your hips back. Twist the adversary wrists in a clockwise motion bringing your hands over your head. Place your left hand on his elbow and bring him down by side stepping. Apply ground control with Uke on stomach 2.

Safety considerations: Simulate the break in class. Uke should bend forward to alleviate any pressure, and signal submission by slapping his side or the mat.

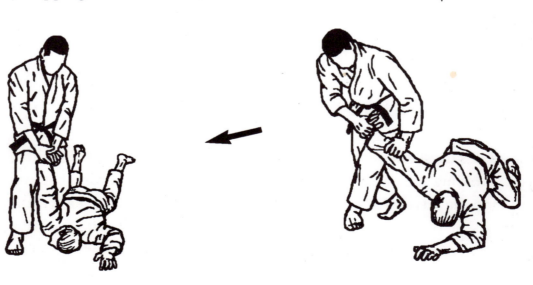

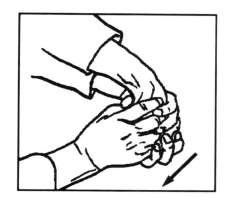

Stationary knife at stomach

The adversary grabs your lapel with his left hand and holds the knife to your stomach with his right hand. Bring your hands up as if surrendering. Suddenly twist your hips 90 degrees clockwise. Cross your thumbs on the back of his hand and pull him forward past your body. Apply compound Kote-gaeshi. Stretch him out and apply a ground control.

Stationary knife at kidney

The adversary holds a knife at your kidney and places his hand around your mouth. Step back with your right leg as you pivot your hips clockwise. Simultaneously bring your right hand down. Brush his right hand away from you and towards him. Reach your right hand around his waist and grab his right shoulder with your left hand. Throw him to his back with Ogoshi. Finish with a ground strike.

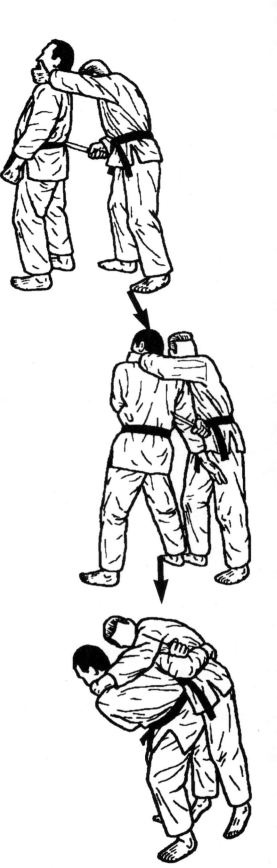

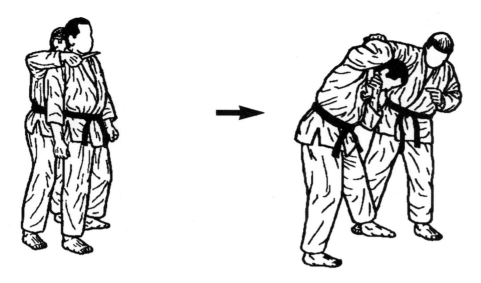

Stationary knife at throat

The adversary holds a knife to your throat with his right hand from behind. Reach up as if you are about to surrender. Grab his right wrist with your left hand and his elbow with your right hand. Pull down sharply. Drive your head under the adversary's armpit. Pivot on your right foot and step back. You should be facing the adversary. The knife edge of his extended hand should face the sky. Drive down and break the adversary's elbow. Side step and bring the adversary to his face.

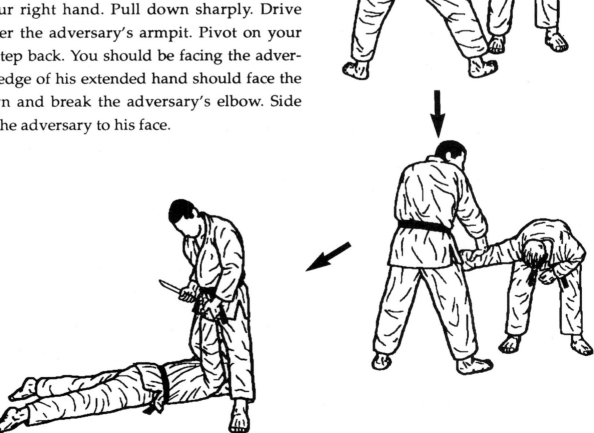

Knife multiple cut

The adversary slashes at your face with a right face cut. Step back with your right leg and lean back, avoiding the slash. The adversary follows with a back hand cut to the face. Execute a block with your left hand to his extended hand. The adversary now attempts to slash your stomach. Block with your left hand to his attacking arm square your hips and give him your stomach as a target. He now withdraws his arm and stabs at your stomach. Pivot 180 degrees and avoid the knife pulling the adversary against your chest. Break the adversary's wrist with Kote-gaeshi and throw him to the ground.

Safety considerations: The Uke takes a free fall to avoid having his wrist dislocated. During the ground control the Uke should signal submission by slapping his side or the mat.

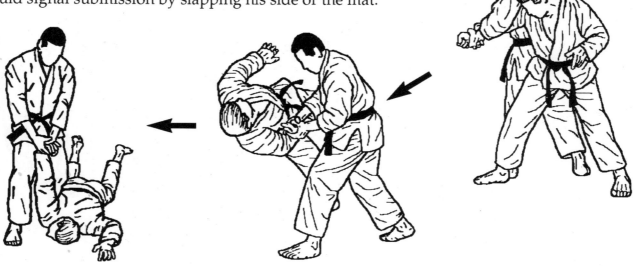

Club overhead Kansetsu waza

The adversary attempts to strike the top of your head with a club. Step forward obliquely with your left leg. Execute a left forearm block to his arm which will be immediately followed by grabbing his right wrist, fingers and thumbs up. Your head should be outside of the path of the club in case your block is unsuccessful. Note that this is not an X block. Execute Kansetsu waza to the adversary's elbow. Apply ground control Uke on stomach 2.

Safety considerations: The adversary should slap his body or the ground to indicate submission.

Club backhand to head Kote-gaeshi

The adversary swings the club to the side of your face. Duck under his swing. The adversary now swings backhand to your face. Step forward with your left foot and block with your right hand. Reach up and break the adversary's wrist with Kote-gaeshi # 8.

Safety considerations: Uke must take a free fall. Note that your knee is pointed down so that if the adversary falls awkwardly on your knee he will not dislocate it.

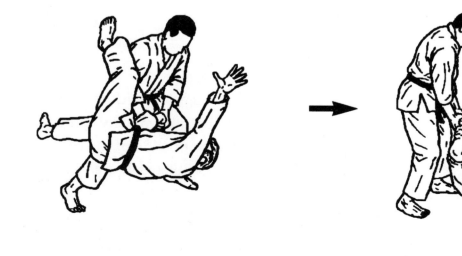

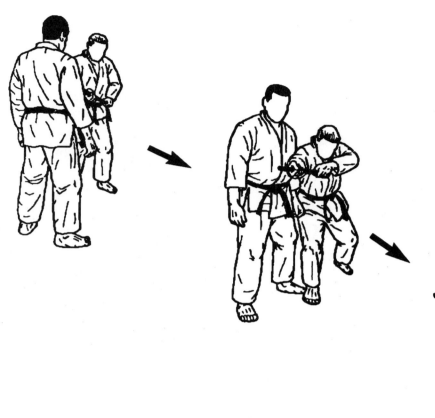

Club stomach thrust corridor

The adversary attacks with a two handed thrust to your midsection. Pivot 180 degrees to the adversary's right side and avoid the attack. Grab the adversary's left hand fingers and thumb down, palm facing towards you, pinning his hand to the stick. Drive the crook of your elbow across the adversary's elbow and grab the middle of the stick with your right hand, palm out. Fracture the adversary's elbow and throw him to his back.

Safety considerations: The adversary must take a free fall.

Club body slap Ude gatame

The adversary attacks with a right sided swing to your body. Step forward into a left front stance and execute a down block. Immediately trap the adversary's right elbow and apply Ude gatame. Pivot 180 degrees and immobilize the adversary.

Safety considerations: The adversary should slap his body or the ground to indicate submission.

Advanced Combat Ju-jutsu Pg 173

Club backhand compound Kote-gaeshi

The adversary swings the club to the side of your face. Step forward slightly, lower your hips and duck under the adversary's swing. The adversary now swings backhand to your body. Step in and grab the adversary's right wrist with your right hand. Strike the adversary's elbow with the crook of your arm thus fracturing it. Bring the adversary's arm on your left shoulder and perform an armbar further injuring the elbow. Drop under the adversary's extended arm and apply compound Kote-gaeshi.

Safety considerations: Simulate the break in class.

Club backhand legs Shiho-nage

The adversary swings backhand to your legs. Pivot 180 degrees on your right leg and execute a down block with your left hand. Reach over with your right hand, cross your thumbs on the back of his hand and pull him forward. Step forward and execute Shiho-nage dislocating his wrist and shoulder. Follow with a ground control.

Gun to forehead Kansetsu waza

The adversary holds a gun to your forehead with his right hand. While bringing your hands up as if surrendering immediately reach up and grab his wrist with both hands. Tilt your head backwards so if the gun fires you will only receive a graze. Step forward and apply Waki-gatame to his elbow. Bring him down by applying pressure towards his elbow. Strip the gun out of his hand by pushing his index finger back toward the back of his hand.

Safety considerations: The Uke should not put his finger on the trigger of the gun because it may be broken during the fall or the disarm.

Gun to stomach Kote-gaeshi

The adversary holds a gun to your stomach. Pivot your waist to the left side so that if he fires a shot you will receive only a graze. The best time to move is when the adversary is distracted, for example when he reaches for your wallet. Grab his gun hand with your left hand. Bring your right hand to meet your left and apply Kote-gaeshi and break the adversary's wrist as you throw him to the ground.

Safety considerations: The Uke must execute a free fall. The Uke should not put his finger on the trigger of the gun because it may be broken during the fall or the disarm.

Gun to back of head tigerlock

The adversary holds a gun with his right hand to the back of your head. Duck your head to the right so that if the gun fires as you are moving you will receive only a graze. Step back with your right leg as you pivot your hips counter clockwise. Simultaneously brush his right hand away from you with your left arm. Execute a tigerlock and throw him to his back with Seoi nage.

Gun to side Kote-gaeshi

The adversary holds a gun with his right hand to your right side. When the adversary reaches for your wallet this is the time to move. Step forward with your left leg and brush his wrist with your right hand. Reach over with your left hand and apply Kote-gaeshi and break the adversary's wrist as you throw him to the ground.

Safety considerations: The Uke should not put his finger on the trigger of the gun because it may be broken during the fall or the disarm.

Adversary reaches for a gun pendulum

The adversary attempts to draw a gun from his waist band. Step forward with your right leg and grab the adversary's right hand. Your thumb should be on the back of his hand and your fingers are draped over the knife edge of his hand. Bring your left hand to meet your right hand fingers crossed on the back of the adversary's hand. Step back with your right leg and execute a pendulum, shattering the adversary's wrist and forcing him to the ground in a front fall. Strip the gun from his hand by applying pressure downwards on the wrist and pinning his arm between your knees.

Variations: This technique can also be done from the adversary reaching for his gun from a side holster or from behind his back.

Pg 180 Advanced Combat Ju-jutsu

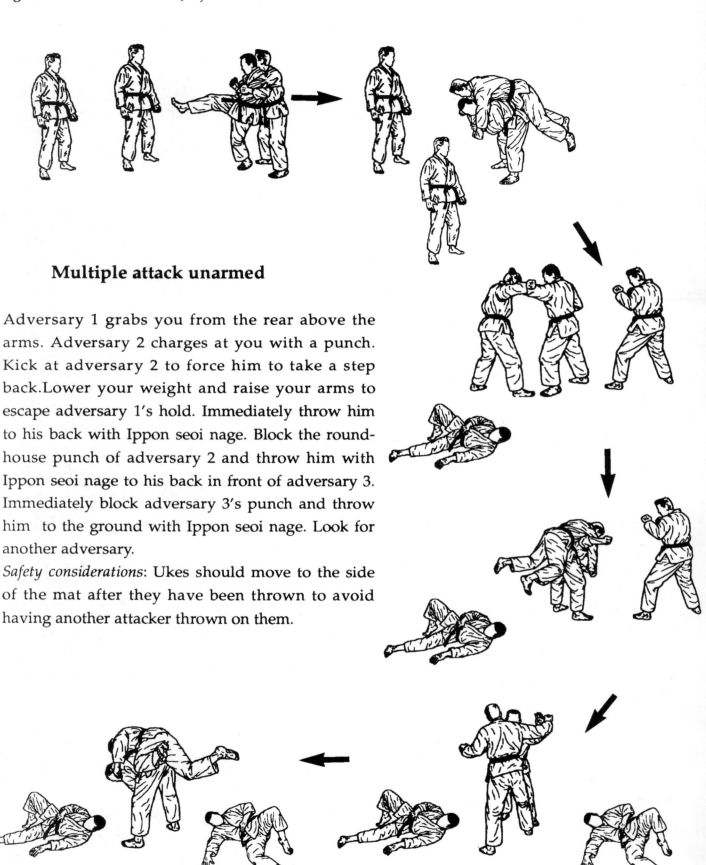

Multiple attack unarmed

Adversary 1 grabs you from the rear above the arms. Adversary 2 charges at you with a punch. Kick at adversary 2 to force him to take a step back. Lower your weight and raise your arms to escape adversary 1's hold. Immediately throw him to his back with Ippon seoi nage. Block the roundhouse punch of adversary 2 and throw him with Ippon seoi nage to his back in front of adversary 3. Immediately block adversary 3's punch and throw him to the ground with Ippon seoi nage. Look for another adversary.

Safety considerations: Ukes should move to the side of the mat after they have been thrown to avoid having another attacker thrown on them.

Aid someone who is attacked

The adversary attempts to stab your partner with a stomach thrust. Quickly reach from behind him with your right forearm and block his attack at the wrist. Grab around his neck with your left arm and place your hand against the side of his cheek to control his head. Brace his right elbow against your chest fracturing the elbow. Pivot on the ball of your left foot and throw the adversary to his back.
Safety considerations: Person who is being attacked should be alert and prepare to move in case the attack is not thwarted.

Front kick Nidan Kosoto-gari

The adversary kicks at your groin with a right front kick. Step forward and turn your hips 90 degrees clockwise. Scoop his outer leg with the crook of your right elbow. Step in and strike Shuto to his jaw reap his left leg and throw him to his back with Kosoto-gari.

Side kick pick up

The adversary attempts a right side kick to your midsection. Step obliquely to your left and avoid the adversary's kick. Reach between the adversary's legs with your right hand and grab the back of his collar with your left Bring the adversary to your chest and throw him face forward to the ground. Apply a ground control.

Advanced Combat Ju-jutsu **Pg 185**

Roundhouse kick Ouchi-gari

The adversary attempts a right roundhouse kick to your head. Step forward with your left leg and raise both hands. Block his extended leg with your forearms. Grab his right leg. Execute Ouchi-gari and finish with a right punch to his groin.

Sitting front choke Kansetsu waza

The adversary grabs you by the neck and attempts to choke you with both hands. Reach up and grab him in a lobster grip. Strike Seiken to his groin. Apply Kansetsu waza, pivot on your right leg and drive him into the chair.

Safety considerations: Uke must use his hands to brace himself so that his head does not hit the chair.

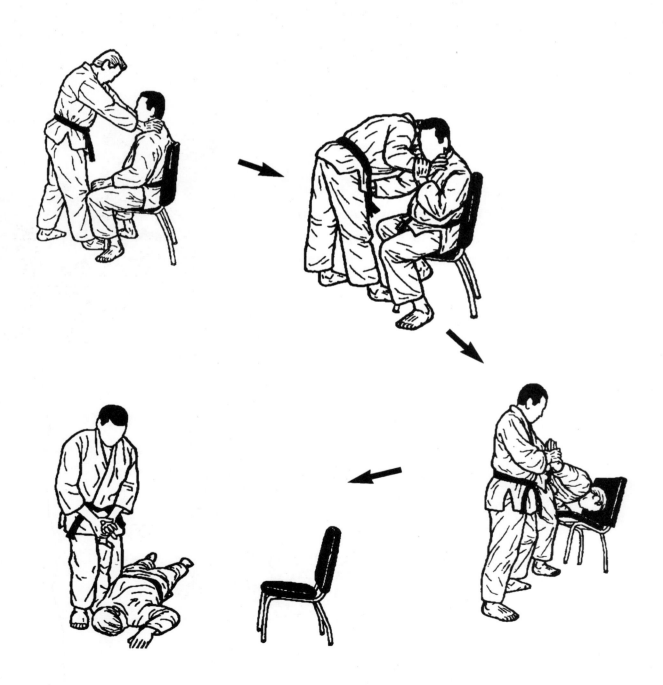

Sitting lapel grab Sankyo

The adversary grabs you by the left lapel and tries to punch you with his right hand. Block his punch. Strike the bend in his right elbow with your right hand and apply Sankyo. Bring him down forward into the chair.

Safety considerations: Uke must use his hands to brace himself so that his head does not hit the chair.

Sitting throat thrust Osoto-gari

Sit in a natural position facing the adversary. As the adversary attacks with a right straight thrust to your chest twist your hips and trunk 90 degrees clockwise. Parry with the right hand against his extended right wrist. Grab his hand with your left hand and place it on your neck. Strike to the bend in the adversary's right elbow with a right forearm off balancing him. Throw him with right sided Osoto-gari reaping his right leg.

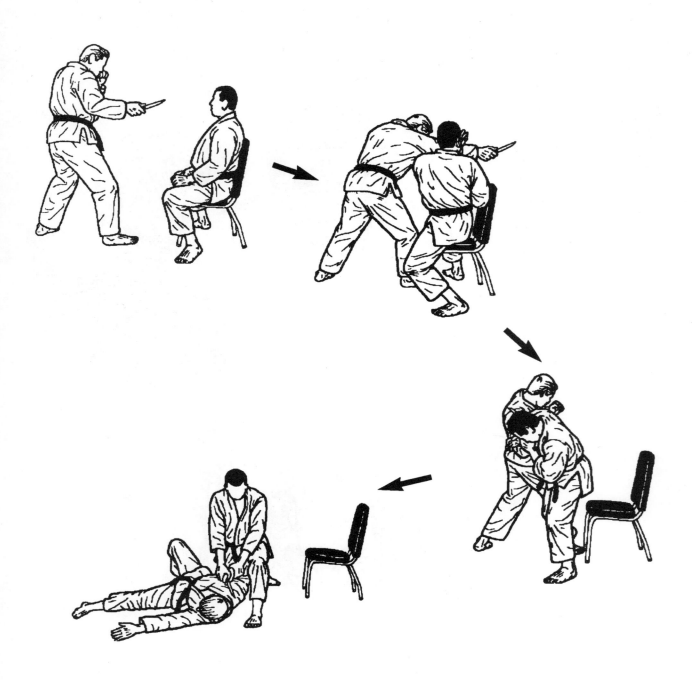

Sitting rear choke Ippon seoi nage

The adversary grabs you from behind around the neck as you are sitting. Grab to the outside of the chair with your left hand. Reach up with your right hand and grab his attacking arm. Bend forward at the waist and turn your shoulders as you pick the adversary up onto your back. Throw him with Ippon seoi nage to the floor. Finish him with a chair strike.

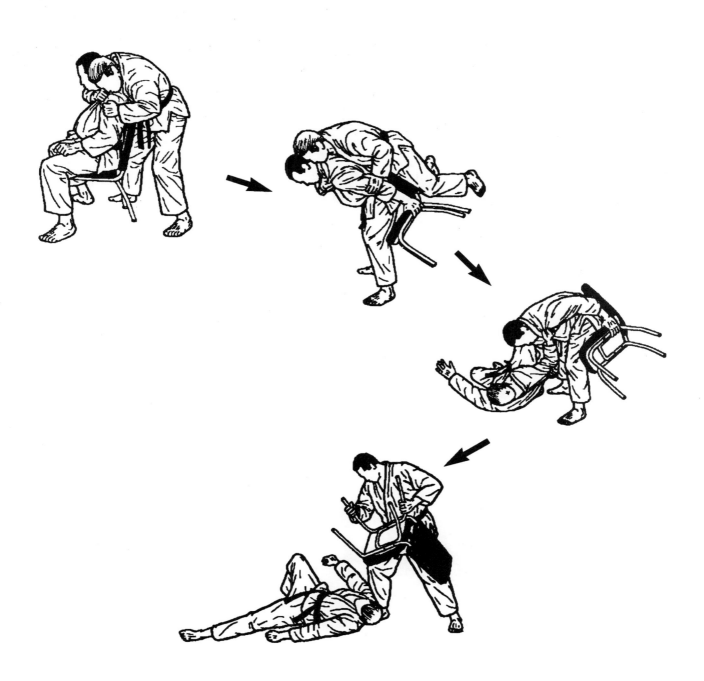

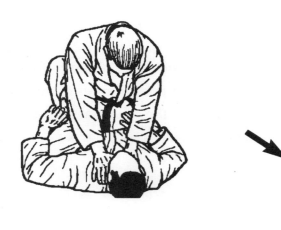

Ground Choke Kansetsu waza

You are lying on your back right knee up. The adversary sits on your stomach and begins to choke you with both hands. Grab his right hand, web up, with your left hand. Strike between his arms to his jaw with a right Shotei. Twist onto your right shoulder as you throw him off of you. Follow up with Kansetsu waza while on the ground.

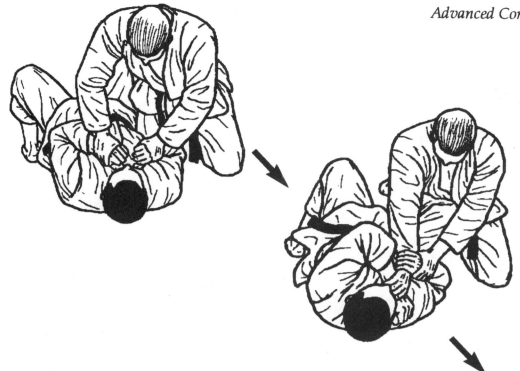

Ground wrist grab Ude Hishigi Juji-gatame

You are lying on your back right knee between yourself and your adversary. He is at your side and has both of your wrists pinned to your chest. Grab his right wrist with your right hand and snatch him toward you. Kick him in the jaw with your left heel as you throw your leg over his shoulder. Pull back with your left leg against his face. Execute Ude hishigi Juji gatame and break his right elbow.

Safety considerations: The Uke should slap the mat repeatedly to indicate submission.

Ground face cut

You are lying on your back right knee up. The adversary attacks from your right side with a face cut. Sit up and block his right forearm with your left hand. Strike with right Koko to his jaw. Rotate your hips 180 degrees and throw him over your body. Continue to turn and straddle his chest finishing him with Kansetsu waza.
Safety considerations: The Uke should slap the mat repeatedly to indicate submission.

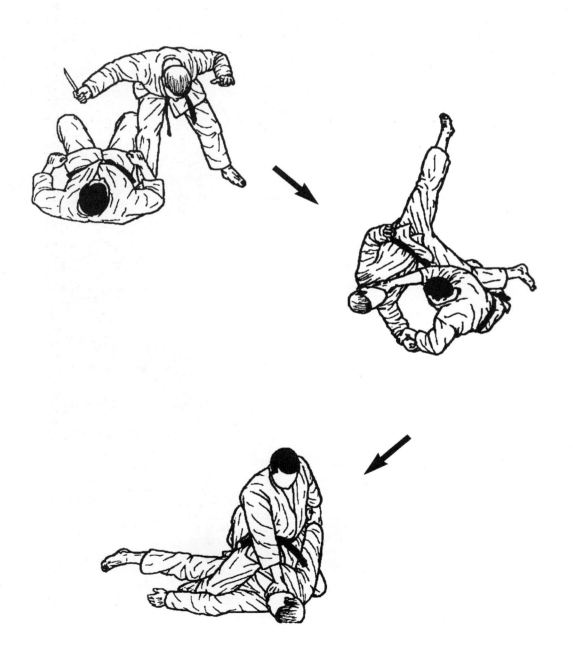

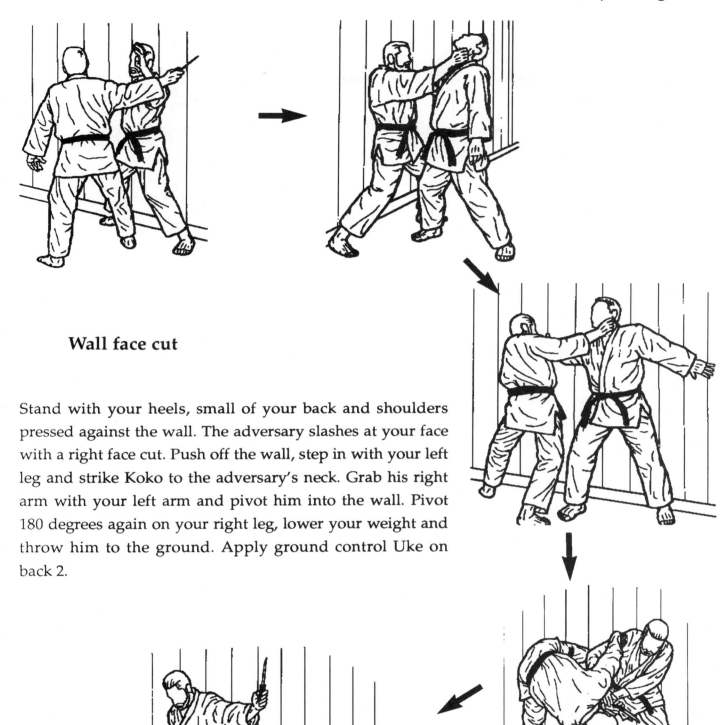

Wall face cut

Stand with your heels, small of your back and shoulders pressed against the wall. The adversary slashes at your face with a right face cut. Push off the wall, step in with your left leg and strike Koko to the adversary's neck. Grab his right arm with your left arm and pivot him into the wall. Pivot 180 degrees again on your right leg, lower your weight and throw him to the ground. Apply ground control Uke on back 2.

Pg 196   Advanced Combat Ju-jutsu

Wall Knife disembowlment Kansetsu waza

Stand with your heels, small of your back and shoulders pressed against the wall. The adversary attempts to disembowel you with an upwards arcing right stab. Squeeze your fingers together and extend them crossing your wrists, right over left. Block the arcing arm between your wrists as your lower your body into a deep horse stance, forcing your hips back. Twist the adversary wrist and apply Kansetsu waza, bringing him to the ground.

Kote gaeshi countered with Kansetsu waza

You attack with a right thrust to the adversary's face. The adversary blocks and attempts Kote-gaeshi 2. Step forward and grab the back of the adversary's wrist with your left hand. Execute Kansetsu waza and drive the adversary to the ground.

Kansetsu waza countered with Sukui nage

You attack with a right thrust to the adversary's face. The adversary blocks cross body block and attempts Kansetsu waza. Bend your right elbow, reach behind his knee and execute Sukuinage.

Tigerlock countered with Ogoshi

You attack with a right roundhouse punch to the adversary's face. The adversary blocks and attempts a tigerlock. As the adversary wraps around your right arm, reach behind his waist and throw the adversary to his back with an Ogoshi.

Hammerlock countered with Koshi-guruma

You attack with a right roundhouse punch to the adversary's face. The adversary blocks and attempts a hammerlock. Turn and strike with a left elbow to the side of his head. Throw him to his back with Koshi-guruma.

Advanced Combat Ju-jutsu **Pg 201**

Devil's handshake countered with Uki waza

You attack with a right roundhouse punch to the adversary's face. The adversary blocks and attempts a devil handshake. As he attempts to grab you and pull you across grab his lapel with your right hand, his elbow with your left and throw him with a right sided Uki waza.

Ippon seoi nage countered with Ogoshi

You attack with a right roundhouse punch to the adversary's face. The adversary blocks and attempts an Ippon seio nage. Place your left hand against his kidney, lower your weight and thrust your hips forward, blocking his throw. Step around him and throw him with left sided Ogoshi.

Osoto-gari countered with Osoto-gari

You attack with a right roundhouse punch to the adversary's face. The adversary blocks and attempts an Osoto-gari. Step back and around on your left leg. Break the adversary's balance to his front, reap his right leg and throw him to his back with Osoto-gari

6th kyu Orange Belt

Time-in-grade: 20 lessons

Total score: 25 points
Passing score: 18 points

1. Formal Bow and Ukemi (5 points)
a. Three sitting, squatting, standing b. Side falls (one hand, two hands) c. Rolls (both sides)

2. Tai Sabaki (1 point)
(Without Uke)
a. Formal b. Escape c. Punishment

3. Kotegaeshi (3 points)
a. 1 through 3 on either side

4. Kansetsuwaza (2 points)
a. Left or right

5. Wrist Grabs (2 points)
a. Double wrist (Kansetsuwaza or Kotegaeshi) b. Single wrist (Kansetsuwaza or Kotegaeshi)

6. Lapel Grabs (2 points)
a. One single hand grab (Kansetsuwaza or Kotegaeshi) b. One double hand grab (Kansetsuwaza or Kotegaeshi)

7. Body Grabs from Behind (1 point)
a. Upper chest grab (Seionage)

8. Mugs (2 points)
a. Around the neck b. Around the neck, one step back

10. Weapons Attacks (3 points)
a. Knife thrust to stomach (Kotegaeshi) b. Face slash (Ippon Seionage) c. Club to the side of the head (Ippon Seionage)

11. Formal Moves (3 points)
a. Ippon Seoi nage b. Koshi-guruma c. Uki Otoshi

12. Conduct, Attendance and Spirit (1 point)

5th kyu Yellow Belt

Time-in-grade: 20 lessons

1. Formal Bow and Ukemi (5 points)
a. Three sitting, squatting, standing b. Side falls (one hand, two hands) c. Rolls (both sides) d. One man obstacle (right and left)

2. Tai Sabaki (7 point)
a. Formal b. Escape c. Punishment

3. Kotegaeshi (4 points)
a. 1 through 4, right and left

4. Kansetsuwaza (2 points)
a. Left and right (Step in, step out)

5. Wrist Grabs (4 points)
a. Double wrist (Kansetsuwaza or Kotegaeshi) b. Single wrist (Kansetsuwaza or Kotegaeshi) c. Cross wrist (Kansetsuwaza or Kotegaeshi) d. Double hand on one wrist (Shuto strike)

6. Lapel Grabs (3 points)
a. One single hand grab (Kansetsuwaza or Kotegaeshi) b. One double hand grab (Kansetsuwaza or Kotegaeshi) c. Single pull close (right and left sides) I. Osotogari II. Ude-garami

7. Body Grabs from Behind (3 point)
a. Upper chest grab (Seionage) b. Lower arms (Sukuinage) c. Under arms (Kansetsuwaza)

8. Mugs (3 points)
a. Around the neck b. Around the neck, one step back c. Around the neck full unbalance

9. Weapons Attacks (6 points)
a. Knife thrust to stomach (Kotegaeshi) b. Face slash (Ippon Seionage) c. Carotid stab (Kotegaeshi) d. Club to the side of the head (Ippon Seionage) e. Club to the top of the head (Kotegaeshi) f. Backhand to the side of the head (Kansetsuwaza)

10 Formal Moves (5 points)
a. Ippon Seionage b. Koshi Guruma c. Uki Otoshi d. Osotogari e. Sukuinage

11. Conduct, Attendance and Spirit (3 points)

Total score: 45 points
Passing score: 35 points

4th kyu Green Belt

Time-in-grade: 32 lessons

1. Formal Bow and Ukemi (5 points)
a. Three sitting, squatting, standing b. Side falls (one hand, two hands) c. Rolls (both sides) d. Two man obstacle (right and left) e. Forward somersault (with and without hands)

2. Tai Sabaki (8 point)
a. Full action b. Question: What is Atemiwaza? c. Question: Name four hand techniques used in Atemiwaza? (Seiken, Uraken, Shuto, Haito)

3. Kotegaeshi (5 points)
a. 1 through 5, right and left

4. Kansetsuwaza (3 points)
a. Single wrist b. Elbow c. Shoulder

5. Wrist Grabs (3 points)
a. Double wrist (Kansetsuwaza and Kotegaeshi) b. Single wrist (Kansetsuwaza and Kotegaeshi) c. Cross wrist (Kansetsuwaza and Kotegaeshi) d. Double hand on one wrist (Shuto strike)

6. Lapel Grabs (5 points)
a. Single hand grab with throws (Ippon Seionage, Ogoshi) b. Double hand grab (Kotegaeshi 3, Kansetsuwaza) c. Single hand cross lapel (Kansetsuwaza) d. Single pull close, right and left sides (Osotogari, Shihonage)

7. Body Grabs from Behind (4 point)
a. Upper chest grab (Seionage) b. Lower arms (Sukuinage) c. Under arms (Ankle pull, double ankle pull)

8. Front Body Grabs (4 points)
a. Front neck embrace (Osotogari) b. Chest embrace (Koshi Guruma) c. Bear hug (Ogoshi) d. Lower arms (Uki Goshi)

9. Mugs (4 points)
a. Around the neck b. Around the neck, one step back c. Around the neck full unbalance d. Flying mare

10. Multiple Attack (2 points)
a. Defend from a two man attack with knife and club in rapid order (Kotegaeshi, Ippon seionage)

11. Knife Attacks (6 points)
a. Knife thrust to stomach (Kotegaeshi) b. Face slash (Ippon Seionage, Harai Goshi) c. Carotid stab (Kotegaeshi, Throat throwback)

12. Club Attacks (6 points)
a. Club to the side of the head (Koshi Guruma, Taiotoshi) b. Club to the top of the head (Kotegaeshi, Throat throwback) c. Backhand to the side of the head (Ude gatame) d. Backhand to the legs (Gyaku Kotegaeshi)

13. Front Chokes (2 points)
a. Two hands on the neck (Kansetsuwaza) b. One hand on the neck (Kotegaeshi 3)

14 Formal Moves (10 points)
a. Ippon Seionage b. Koshi Guruma c Uki otoshi. d. Osotogari e. Sukuinage f. Kosotogari. g. Ogoshi h. Uki Goshi i. Ju-jutsu Taiotoshi j. Harai Goshi

11. Conduct, Attendance and Spirit (3 point)

Total score: 70 points
Passing score: 50 points

Pg 208 Advanced Combat Ju-jutsu

3rd kyu Brown Belt

Time-in-grade: 6 months

1. Formal Bow and Ukemi (6 points)
a. What is the meaning of Ukemi?
b. Demonstrate Ukemi:
1. Three sitting, squatting, standing 2. Side falls (one hand, two hands) 3. Forward somersault (with and without hands) 4. Rolls (left/right) 5. Back rolls (left/right) 6. Dead front fall 7. Side seperation (left/right) 8. Free fall roll 9. Kotegaeshi rolls (left/right) 10. 3 man obstacle.

2. Tai Sabaki (10 points)
a. What is the meaning of Tai sabaki?
b. Can you switch from one to another? c. Formal d. Escape e. Punishment (Seiken) f. Uraken g. Preparation kicks h. With throws.

3. Kotegaeshi (6 points)
a. What is the meaning of Kote-gaeshi?
b. 1 through 6 (right and left)

4. Kansetsu waza (3 points)
a. What is the meaning of Kansetsu waza?
b. Demonstrate Kansetsu waza (left/right):
1. Basic, stepping in, stepping back 2. Stepping in, stepping in 3. Stepping in, stepping in to produce wrist punishment 4. Stepping in, stepping back to produce wrist punishment 5. Double wrist grab 6. Double elbow grab.

5. Wrist Grabs and pendulums (15 points)
a. Four double b. Four single, same side c. four cross wrist d. Three double hand on one wrist e. Pendulum to the rear and to the front.

6. Lapel Grabs (10 points)
a. Three double with out-twisted hands b. Three double stiff armed c. Two lapel bent arm pull close (left and right) d. One cross lapel, pull around (left and right)

7. Front Body Grabs (4 points)
a. Front neck embrace (Osotogari) b. Chest embrace (Ogoshi) c. Lower arms (Uki-goshi) d. Under arms (Koshi-guruma)

8. Body Grabs from Behind (6 points)
a. Two upper arms b. Two lower arms c. Two under arms

9. Mugs (5 points)
1 a. Around the neck b. Around the neck, one step back c. Around the neck full unbalance d. Flying mare e. Knee in back.
2 Resisting mug

10. Chokes (6 points)

a. Two from the front
b. Two from the side
c. Two from the rear

11. Rapid Order Attack (2 points)

From mug #1, same man attacks with a looping right hand after having been thrown.

12. Multiple Attack (3 points)
Three man attack (knife, club, punch)

13. Knife Attacks (12 points)
a. Three knife thrust to stomach b. Three face slashes c. Three carotid stabs d. One looping right body slash e. One backhand to the face f. One throat thrust

14. Club Attacks (7 points)
a. Three club to the left side of the head b. One club to the right side of the head with the left hand. c. Two to the top of the head d. One to the shins, backhand e. One backhand to the head.

15. Aid Someone Being Attacked (2 points)
a. Knife thrust to stomach b. Stick to the side of the head

3rd kyu Brown Belt

16. Formal Moves (16 points)
1. Ippon Seoi nage 2. Koshi-guruma 3 Uki otoshi. 4. Osotogari 5. Sukuinage 6. Kosotogari. 7. Ogoshi 8. Uki-goshi 9. Jujutsu Tai otoshi 10. Harai-goshi 11. Judo Tai otoshi 12. Yama arashi (2 ways) 13. Ouchi-gari 14. Kouchi-gari 15. Morote Seoi nage 16. Tomoe nage.

17. Conduct, Attendance and Spirit (8 points)

18. Extra points (5 points)
Club Affiliation_____

19. Tanjo jutsu Basics (30 points)
1. Formal bow (1 point)
2. Tai sabaki 1 man attack (5 points)
3. Tai sabaki with throws (5 points)
4. Taisabaki wipe away (10 points)
a. Without punishment b. With punishment
5. Knife attacks (5 points)
a. Face cut b. Knife thrust
6. Grabs (4 points, left and right)
a. Wrist grab b. Tanjo grab c. Single lapel grab d. Double lapel grab.

With Tanjo
Total score: 150 points
Passing score: 110 points

Without Tanjo
Total score: 120 points
Passing score: 95 points

2nd kyu Brown Belt

Time-in-grade: 6 months

1. Formal Bow (2 points)
What is the logic behind the formal Ju-jutsu bow?

2. Ukemi (4 points)
a. What is the meaning of Ukemi?
b. Demonstrate Ukemi:
1. Three sitting, squatting, standing 2. Side falls (one hand, two hands) 3. Forward somersault (with and without hands) 4. Rolls (left/right) 5. Back rolls (left/right) 6. Dead front fall 7. Side separation (left/right) 8. Free fall roll 9. Kotegaeshi rolls (left/right) 10. 4 man obstacle.

3. Tai Sabaki (10 points)
a. What is the meaning of Tai sabaki?
b. Can you switch from one to another? c. Formal d. Escape e. Punishment (Seiken) f. Uraken g. Preparation kicks h. With throws i. To the rear j. To the rear with throws

4. Kotegaeshi & Pendulums (19 points)
a. 1 through 8 (right & left)
b. Pendlum to the rear (right & left)
c. Pendulum to the side (right & left)
d. Pendulum to the front (right & left)

5. Kansetsu waza from formal (8 points)
a. Basic, stepping in, stepping back b. Stepping in, stepping in c. Stepping in, stepping in to produce wrist punishment d. Stepping in, stepping back to produce wrist punishment

6. Kansetsu waza with speed (4 points)
a. Double wrist b. Double elbow c. Double outer shoulder d. Double upper shoulder

7. Kote-gaeshi with speed (3 points)
a. Both wrists grabbed b. Both elbows grabbed c. Both outer shoulders grabbed.

8. Devils handshake & Tigerlock (4 pts)
a. Demonstrate Devil's Handshake (with and without clothes) from a looping punch to the head and ending with a throw.
b. Demonstrate Tigerlock (with & without clothes) from a looping punch to the head and ending with a throw.

9. Wrist Grabs (16 points)
a. Four single on the right wrist b. Four single on the left wrist. c. Four single cross wrist, left or right d. Four double cross wrist grabs, left or right

10. Come Alongs (6 pts)
a. 3 simple b. 3 bonelocks

11. Lapel Grabs (9 points)
a. Three double b. Three single c. Three double, pull close

12. Body Grabs from Behind (6 points)
a. Two upper arms b. Two lower arms
c. Two under arms

13. Front Body Grabs (4 points)
a. Front neck embrace (Osotogari, Ogoshi) b. Chest embrace (Harai goshi, Uki-goshi) c. Lower arms (Uki-goshi, Ogoshi) d. Under arms (Koshi-guruma)

14. Mugs (8 points)
1 (Right and left) a. Around the neck b. Around the neck, one step back c. Around the neck full unbalance d. Flying mare e. Knee in back.
2. (Right side only) a. Hand over mouth pull back b. Hair pull c. Full unbalance (Ouchi, Kouchi)

15 Pressure points (20 points)
Articulate an point out pressure points on both sides of the body (front and back)

2nd kyu Brown Belt

16. Multiple Attack (4 points)
a. Simulate (with speed) a defense from a 4 man unarmed attack.

17. Multiple Attack (4 points)
a. Simulate (with speed) a defense from a 4 man attack who have a knife, a club, one who punches and from a back body grab.

18. Kick Defense (5 pts)
a. Four front kicks b. A kick to the body while lying on the stomach

19. Force a person to stand from a sitting position (2 pts)
a. Use head pressure points two ways.

20. Wall techniques (20 points)
a. Two groin stabs b. Two stomach thrust c. Two carotids d. Two face slashes e. Two backhands to the face

21. Single Man Rapid Order Knife attack (4 pts)
Uke attacks with a face slash, backhand slash, left side body slash and a stomach thrust

22. Club Attacks (10 points)
With speed and applying a different technique to each attack, defend from:
a. Two to the left side of the head b. Two club to the right side of the head with the left hand. c. Two to the top of the head d. One right backhand body slash e. One right backhand to the legs. f. One right hand to the legs.

23. Aid Someone Being Attacked (2 points)
a. A carotid knife attack b. A face slash.

24. Goshin Jutsu (7pts)
Demonstrate the first seven moves of the Goshin jutsu.

25. Promotion procedures
Respond to random questions on the promotion procedures

26. Formal Moves (22 points)
1. Ippon Seoi nage 2. Koshi-guruma 3 Uki otoshi. 4. Osotogari 5. Sukuinage 6. Kosotogari. 7. Ogoshi 8. Uki-goshi 9. Ju-jutsu Tai otoshi 10. Harai-goshi 11. Judo Tai otoshi 12. Yama arashi (2 ways) 13. Ouchi-gari 14. Kouchi-gari 15. Morote Seoi nage 16. Tomoe nage. 17. Uki waza 18. Osoto-guruma 19. Kata-guruma 20. Sode tsuri komi-goshi 21. Soto Makikomi (3 ways) 22. Tsuri-goshi

27. Jo-jutsu Katas #1 (2 points)

28. Bokken katas #1 and #2 (4 points)

29. Tanjo jutsu (10 points)

30. Spirit, attitude & attendance (7pts)

31. Extra credit
Proper uniform dress (add or deduct 5 pts)
Contribution to the Ryu (add or deduct 5 pts)

Total score: 224 points
Passing score: 168 points

1st kyu Brown Belt

Time-in-grade: 6 months

1. General knowledge
a. What is the meaning of Miyama Ryu?
b. Why that name?
c. From whom it and where did it originate?
d. What is Ukemi?
e. Tell the difference in the arts (Judo, Ju-jutsu, Aikido, and Karate)
f. Demonstrate all types of Ukemi (Judo, Ju-jutsu, and Aikido)
g. Demonstrate Ippon Seoi nage in the Judo form and then in the Ju-jutsu form.

2. Tai Sabaki
a. What is the meaning of Tai sabaki?
b. How many does Miyama use?
c. Can you switch from one to another?
d. Demonstrate all your Tai sabaki defenses.
1. Formal 2. Escape 3. Punishment (Seiken) 4. Uraken 5. Kicking 6. Cat step escapes 7. With throws 8. To the rear 9. To the rear with throws

3. Pressure points
a. Articulate and point out 21 pressure points on both sides of the body (front and back)
b. What are pressure points mainly used for?

4. Vital areas
a. Show and name 14 vital areas on the front and back of the body.
b. What are the vital areas mainly used for?
c. Under what circumstances would you strike for a vital area?

5. Atemi Waza
a. What is the meaning of Atemi waza?
b. Demonstrate Atemi to the Vital areas:
1. Four open hand strike giving Japanese names 2. Three different ways with the closed fist giving Japanese names 3. Three distinct ways with the foot 4. Name six parts of the leg used for Atemi. Name eight parts of the arm used for Atemi.

6. Come Alongs
Demonstrate six simple and six bonelocks.

7. Mugs
1 Around the neck 2. Around the neck, one step back 3. Around the neck full unbalance 4. Flying mare 5. Knee in back 6. Hand over mouth pull back 7. Hair pull 8. Full unbalance (Ouchi, Kouchi) 9. Ouster 10. Sleeper hold 11. Full Nelson 12. Half nelson 13. Walking mug 14. Neck grab (Aiki kneeling 15. Neck grab (Goshin jutsu) 16 Neck grab (Scoop back of heel with instep 17. Front knee dislocation.

8. Body Grabs from Behind
a. Two upper arms b. Two lower arms
c. Two under arms

9. Front Body Grabs
a. Front neck embrace (Osotogari, Ogoshi) b. Chest embrace (Harai goshi, Uki-goshi) c. Lower arms (Uki-goshi, Ogoshi) d. Under arms (Koshi-guruma)

10. Wrist Grabs
Demonstrate all your wrist grabs. (minimum of ten moves)

11. Kotegaeshi, Kansetsu waza and Reverses
a. One through eight (right & left) b. Enter into hammerlock four different ways c. Demonstrate Devil's Handshake with and without clothing d. Reverse Kote-gaeshi two different ways e. Reverse Tigerlock using Ogoshi f. Reverse Devil's Handshake using Uki Waza g. Reverse Hammerlock using Koshi-guruma or harai-goshi h. Reverse Kansetsuwaza using Sukuinage i. Reverse Ippon Seoi nage j. Reverse Ogoshi

12. Lapel Grabs
Demonstrate all your defenses from lapel grabs (minimum of 10 moves)

1st kyu Brown Belt

13. Defending From a Seated Position
a. Looping right punch (with or without lapel grab) b. Douple lapel grab, pull c. Single lapel grab, pull d. Double hand choke e. Rear right forearm choke f. Knife thrust to the chest g. Face slash h Backhand face slash

14. Multiple Attack
a. Defend from four men who are unarmed. Start with your arms pinned from the rear.
b. Defend from a 4 man attack against attackers who have a knife, a club, one who punches and from a back body grab.

15. Kick Defense
a. Defend from four front kicks

16. Controls
How many controls can you demonstrate after the attacker has been thrown to the ground.

17. Knife attacks
1. Standing: Oblique slash to the face, backhand to the face, side body slash, stomach thrust 2. Lying: a. Body thrust b. Upper body slash c. Down stab carotid 3. Stationary: a. Knife point held to the stomach b. Knife to the kidneys with left arm around the neck c. Blade to the neck with left hand on hair pull 4. Show all the knife techniques that you have been taught (Show a minimum of 10 moves)

18. Clubs
Demonstrate all your club defenses (show a minimum of 10 moves)

19. Pistol
a. To the forehead b. To the stomach c. To the side of the body d. To the upper back e. To the lower back

Question 20A: Males - Demonstrate the last eight moves of the Miyama Ryu Gokyo moving
a. Hane-goshi b. Hane makikomi c. Uchi mata d. Hiza-guruma e. Sasae Tsurikomi ashi f. Ushiro-goshi g. Hasamae-gaeshi h. Ushiro-guruma.

Females - Female techniques

21. Goshin Jutsu
Demonstrate the first fifteen moves of the Goshin jutsu.

22. Nage No Kata
Demonstrate the first six moves of the Nage no kata left and right

23. Gokkyo No Waza
Demonstrate the first principle of the Kodokan Judo Gokyo No Waza

24. Jodo/Bokkendo
a. Jo-jutsu Katas 1 and 2 b.Bokken katas 1 through 3

25. Tanjo jutsu

26. Spirit, attitude & attendance

27. Extra credit
Proper uniform dress (add or deduct 5 pts)
Contribution to the Ryu (add or deduct 5 pts)

28: Free fighting
a. Karate vs Ju-jutsu b. Judo Randori

Total score: 120 points
Passing score: 102 points

Miyama Ryu Gokyo

White to Orange Belt
1. Ippon Seoi nage
2. Koshi-guruma
3 Uki otoshi.

Orange to Yellow Belt
4. Osotogari
5. Sukuinage

Yellow to Green Belt
6. Kosotogari.
7. Ogoshi
8. Uki-goshi
9. Ju-jutsu Tai otoshi
10. Harai-goshi

Green to 3rd Brown Belt
11. Judo Tai otoshi
12. Yama arashi (2 ways)
13. Ouchi-gari
14. Kouchi-gari
15. Morote Seoi nage
16. Tomoe nage.

3rd Brown to Second Brown
17. Uki waza
18. Osoto-guruma
19. Kata-guruma
20. Sode tsuri komi-goshi
21. Soto Makikomi (3 ways)
22. Tsuri-goshi

2nd Brown to 1st Brown
23. Hane-goshi
24. Hane makikomi
25. Uchi mata
26. Hiza-guruma
27. Sasae Tsurikomi ashi
28. Ushiro-goshi
29. Hasamae-gaeshi
30. Ushiro-guruma.

Okuiri (Entrance to Secrets)

General Requirements:

1. Unquestioned moral character and maturity.
2. Continued practice and interest.
3. Increased proficiency in all lower rank requirements.
4. Terminology and translation for techniques required for lower ranks.
5. Names, colors and order of Miyama Ryu Ju-jutsu ranking system.
6. Teaching grade in the lower ranks.
7. Time-in-Grade: A minimum of six months active since the last promotion.

Ability to demonstrate:

Nage No Kata 1-15 left and right side

Kodokan Gokyo No Waza pricnciples 1 and 2

Tanjo-jutsu

Jo-jutsu katas 1-3

Bokken katas 1-4

Goshin -jutsu (males)

Joshi Goshin-Ho (females)

Moku Roku (Catalouge)

General Requirements:

1. Unquestioned moral character and maturity.
2. Continued practice and interest.
3. Increased proficiency in all lower rank requirements.
4. Terminology and translation for techniques required for lower ranks.
5. Names, colors and order of Miyama Ryu Ju-jutsu ranking system.
6. Teaching grade in the lower ranks.
7. Time-in-Grade: A minimum of two and a half years active since the last promotion.

Ability to demonstrate:

Nage No Kata 1-15 left and right side

Kodokan Gokyo No Waza pricnciples 1 through 3

Kime No Kata (males)

Tanjo-jutsu

Jo-jutsu katas 1-5

Bokken katas 1-10

Goshin -jutsu (males)

Joshi Goshin-Ho (females)

Menkyo (Teacher's license)

General Requirements:

1. Unquestioned moral character and maturity.
2. Continued practice and interest.
3. Increased proficiency in all lower rank requirements.
4. Terminology and translation for techniques required for lower ranks.
5. Names, colors and order of Miyama Ryu Ju-jutsu ranking system.
6. Teaching grade in the lower ranks.
7. Time-in-Grade: A minimum of three years active since the last promotion.

Ability to demonstrate:

Nage No Kata 1-15 left and right side

Kodokan Gokyo No Waza principles 1 through 4 (males)

Kodokan Gokyo No Waza principles 1 through 5 (females)

Kime No Kata (males)

Tanjo-jutsu

Jo-jutsu katas 1-5

Bokken katas 1-10

Goshin -jutsu (males)

Joshi Goshin-Ho (females)

Kime Shike (females)

Kaiden (Everything Passed)

General Requirements:

1. Unquestioned moral character and maturity.
2. Continued practice and interest.
3. Increased proficiency in all lower rank requirements.
4. Terminology and translation for techniques required for lower ranks.
5. Names, colors and order of Miyama Ryu Ju-jutsu ranking system.
6. Teaching grade in the lower ranks.
7. Time-in-Grade: A minimum of five years active since the last promotion.

Ability to demonstrate:

Nage No Kata 1-15 left and right side

Kodokan Gokyo No Waza principles 1 through 5

Koshiki No Kata

Itsutsu No Kata

Kime No Kata (males)

Tanjo-jutsu

Jo-jutsu katas 1-6

Bokken katas 1-12

Goshin -jutsu (males)

Joshi Goshin-Ho (females)

Kime Shike (females)

Ju No Kata (Females)

Black Belt Register

Miyama Ryu Black Belt Register 10/30/93

BB#	Name	Rank	Rank Date	Comments
1	Pablo Martinez	Menkyo	10-27-90	
2	George Klett	Dai Shihan	10-30-93	
3	Vincent Mandina	Mokuroku	06-24-66	
4	William Marquez	Kaiden	10-27-90	
5	Kenneth Winthrop	Okuiri	12-10-65	
6	Miguel A. Lozada	Menkyo	06-03-89	
7	Gene Peluso	Okuiri	06-24-66	
8	Arthur Forstrom	Kaiden	10-28-77	Retired
9	Anthony Chiera	Okuiri	06-24-66	
10	Ralph Reyes	Kaiden	10-27-90	
11	Donald Mestanza	Okuiri	06-24-66	
12	Richard Lazarus	Okuiri	12-23-66	
13	Ted Ielardi	Menkyo	06-03-89	
14	Valerio Chiera	Okuiri	06-30-67	
15	Victor Tozzo	Mokuroku	05-24-70	
16	Patricia Filaoro	Okuiri	06-30-67	
17	David Silverman	Okuiri	06-30-67	
18	Mario Gil	Menkyo	04-27-73	Retired
19	Dr. Lenore Pereira Niles	Okuiri	12-20-67	
20	Eli Nivin	Okuiri	12-20-67	
21	John Scifo	Okuiri	12-20-67	
22	Filiberto Rodriguez	Okuiri	12-20-67	Deceased, 1976
23	Americo Questell	Okuiri	12-20-67	
24	Lewis Palzer	Kaiden	06-22-91	
25	Herman Olaizola	Okuiri	04-26-68	
26	Eric Duran	Okuiri	04-26-68	
27	Gerald Cheers	Mokuroku	04-30-71	
28	Gloria Scifo Alvarez	Menkyo	10-28-77	Retired
29	Marie Lasorella	Okuiri	04-26-68	
30	Helen Wrenn Nishiyama	Okuiri	10-25-68	
31	John Prato	Okuiri	10-25-68	
32	Cecil Greaves	Okuiri	10-25-68	
33	Charles Raineri	Menkyo	04-27-73	
34	John Mascunana	Okuiri	04-25-69	
35	Ted Plonchak	Okuiri	04-25-69	
36	Donald Mackintosh	Okuiri	10-24-69	
37	Santos Martinez	Okuiri	10-24-69	
38	Laiddon Griffith	Okuiri	04-24-70	
39	Michael Alvarez	Kaiden	10-28-77	Retired
40	Jose Sierra	Menkyo	04-30-76	
41	Charles Littlejohn	Okuiri	04-24-70	
42	Israel Diaz	Menkyo	06-03-89	
43	Victor Manuel Pagan	Mokuroku	04-27-73	

Black Belt Register

BB#	Name	Rank	Rank Date	Comments
44	Nelson Andujar	Okuiri	10-30-70	
45	Frederick Rosario	Menkyo	06-03-89	
46	Jorge L. Medina	Okuiri	04-30-71	
47	Manuel Freitas	Okuiri	10-29-71	
48	Raymond Estrella	Kaiden	10-30-81	Deceased, 3-25-82
49	Benjamin Estrella	Kaiden	04-29-83	
50	Ronald Butt	Okuiri	10-29-71	
51	Ralph Rivera	Mokuroku	10-25-74	
52	Glenn M. Victor	Okuiri	10-29-71	
53	Ernest Rhodes	Okuiri	04-27-73	
54	Manuel Ponce	Kaiden	10-14-83	
55	Felix Acevedo	Okuiri	04-27-73	
56	Francisco Ramos	Okuiri	04-27-73	
57	John Wheaton	Menkyo	10-27-78	
58	William Stapleton	Okuiri	04-27-73	Deceased, 12/77
59	Raymond Alvarez	Kaiden	10-14-83	Deceased, 6/85
60	Alonzo Watson	Okuiri	04-27-73	
61	Claudio Lope	Okuiri	04-27-73	
62	Hector M. Negron	Kaiden	10-30-81	
63	Ralph Mazzaro	Okuiri	04-27-73	Honorary Okuiri
64	Hector Torres	Okuiri	04-27-73	
65	Eula Salisbury	Mokuroku	10-28-77	Deceased, 3/88
66	Rafael Reyes	Okuiri	10-26-73	
67	Leonard Jones	Okuiri	10-26-73	Deceased, 6/86
68	Robert Alff	Okuiri	10-26-73	
69	Dolores McHarris	Okuiri	10-26-73	
70	David McHarris	Okuiri	10-26-73	
71	Jose Amato	Kaiden	10-23-87	
72	Diana Dunbar	Okuiri	10-26-73	
73	Dr. John J. Lewis	Kaiden	06-03-89	
74	Rupert William	Mokuroku	04-30-78	
75	Noemi Leal	Mokuroku	10-27-78	
76	Bienvenido Mena	Okuiri	10-25-74	
77	Laura Amato Ponce	Okuiri	10-25-74	
78	Jose A. Ramos	Okuiri	10-25-74	
79	Eloy Carmoega Jr.	Okuiri	10-25-74	
80	Matthew S. Dorfman	Okuiri	10-25-74	
81	Franklin I. Murray	Okuiri	04-25-75	
82	Robert Bassolino	Okuiri	04-25-75	
83	James A. (Carter) Outlaw	Okuiri	04-25-75	
84	Pascual Torres	Okuiri	04-25-75	
85	Roderick A. Senior	Okuiri	04-25-75	
86	Harley Stewart	Okuiri	10-31-75	
87	Michael Paradiso	Okuiri	10-31-75	

Advanced Combat Ju-jutsu Pg 222

Black Belt Register

BB#	Name	Rank	Rank Date	Comments
88	Beatrice Vetsch	Okuiri	10-31-75	
89	Lee Martinez	Okuiri	04-30-76	
90	Irvin Aviles	Okuiri	04-30-76	
91	Otis Harris Sr.	Okuiri	04-30-76	
92	Jose A. Miguel	Okuiri	04-30-76	
93	Hector Cruz	Okuiri	04-30-76	
94	Angel Figueroa	Okuiri	10-29-76	
95	Robert D. Windley	Okuiri	10-29-76	
96	Reinaldo Rivera	Okuiri	04-26-74	
97	Peggy Santiago	Okuiri	04-29-77	
98	William Ocasio	Okuiri	04-29-77	
99	Dr. Abigail Durruthy	Kaiden	11-11-89	
100	Leonard Holmes	Menkyo	04-29-83	Police Club Okuiri
101	Robert E. Magliari	Okuiri	04-29-77	Police Club Graduate
102	Winston Rouse	Okuiri	04-29-77	Police Club Graduate
103	Gene Jerome James	Menkyo	04-29-83	
104	Jose Torres	Menkyo	10-23-87	
105	Pedro Stephen	Okuiri	04-28-78	
106	Miguel Ibarra	Mokuroku	04-24-81	
107	Edwin Lugo	Okuiri	04-28-78	
108	Alfred Vazquez	Mokuroku	10-24-86	
109	Nestor Arce	Okuiri	04-28-78	
110	John Castro	Okuiri	04-28-78	
111	Rocco Campanella	Okuiri	10-27-78	
112	Ronald Siverls	Okuiri	10-27-78	Police Club Graduate
113	Sandra Colon	Menkyo	04-27-84	
114	Oliver Lee	Okuiri	10-27-78	
		3rd Dan	04-24-87	Tae Kwon Do
115	Raymond Campbell	Kaiden	11-11-89	
116	Francisco Ayala Jr.	Okuiri	10-27-78	Police Club Graduate
117	Vivian Jaume	1st Dan	10-27-78	Tae Kwon Do
118	Virginia Cruz	Menkyo	10-27-90	
119	Curtiss Inniss	Menkyo	11-8-85	
		4th Dan	04-24-87	Tae Kwon Do
120	Comstock V. Harding	Okuiri	04-29-79	
121	Dale Lloyd	Kaiden	04-25-92	
122	Louis Rodriguez	Okuiri	04-29-79	Police Club Graduate
123	Vincent Francis Sr.	Okuiri	10-26-79	Police Club Graduate
124	Anthony Netto	Okuiri	10-26-79	Police Club Graduate
125	Adam Victor	Okuiri	10-26-79	Police Club Graduate
126	Edwin Ramirez	Okuiri	10-26-79	
127	Anthony Rodriguez	Okuiri	04-25-80	
128	Joseph Cartagena	Okuiri	04-25-80	
129	Frank B. Smith	Okuiri	04-25-80	

Advanced Combat Ju-jutsu Pg 223

Black Belt Register

BB#	Name	Rank	Rank Date	Comments
130	Keith E. Thomas	Okuiri	04-25-80	
131	Nelson Serrano	Mokuroku	10-19-84	
132	Joseph Fields	Okuiri	04-25-80	
133	George Cruz	Okuiri	04-25-80	
134	David Lopez	Mokuroku	04-27-84	
135	Freebbie Rivera	Okuiri	04-25-80	
136	Benny Pagan	Okuiri	04-25-80	
137	Demetrio Rodriguez	Okuiri	10-31-80	
138	Demetrios A. Milliaressis	Kaiden	11-11-89	Police Club Graduate
139	Peter A. Toro	Okuiri	10-31-80	Police Club Graduate
140	Alberto Garcia	Okuiri	10-31-80	
141	John Ferri	Okuiri	10-31-80	
142	John T. Marchione	Okuiri	10-31-80	
143	Joel S.G. Ross	Okuiri	10-31-80	
144	Harry Young	Okuiri	04-24-81	
145	Candida Soto de Camacho	Kaiden	10-30-93	
146	Natalie Roman	Okuiri	04-24-81	
147	Robert Aviles Sr.	Kaiden	04-25-92	
148	John Bombache	Mokuroku	10-19-84	
149	Jesus Gonzalez Jr.	Menkyo	04-25-92	
150	Miguel Hernandez Jr.	1st Dan	04-24-81	Tae Kwon Do
151	Hector Camacho Jr.	Okuiri	10-30-81	
152	William H. Young	Okuiri	10-30-81	
153	Omyra Santos	Okuiri	10-30-81	
154	Irene Laboy	Okuiri	10-30-81	
155	Leon B. Ellis	Okuiri	10-30-81	
156	Pamela Rodriguez	1st Dan	10-30-81	Tae Kwon Do
157	Lionel D. Nelms	Okuiri	10-30-81	
158	John Wheaton III	Okuiri	10-30-81	
159	Vincent Brusco	Okuiri	10-30-81	Police Club Graduate
160	Dr. William Duke	Kaiden	10-24-92	Santo Domingo, D.R.
161	Eddy Nolasco Sanchez	Kaiden	10-30-93	Santo Domingo, D.R.
162	Edwin M. Vasquez	Okuiri	04-30-82	
163	Luis Alemar	Menkyo	10-26-91	
164	Roy Goldberg	Okuiri	04-30-82	
165	Antonia Veronica Goodell	Okuiri	04-30-82	
166	Jorge Andion	Okuiri	04-29-83	
167	Rafael Medina	Kaiden	10-30-93	Santo Domingo, D.R.
168	Darius G. Chagnon	Okuiri	10-14-83	Northwestern University
169	Edward F. Sullivan	Menkyo	10-24-92	DePaul University
170	Don King	Okuiri	04-29-83	
171	Norberto DiVietro	Okuiri	01-26-83	Santo Domingo, D.R.
172	Rolando Perez	Mokuroku	07-16-88	Santo Domingo, D.R.
173	Carl Daniels	Menkyo	11-11-89	

Black Belt Register

BB#	Name	Rank	Rank Date	Comments
174	Jose Alvarez	Okuiri	10-14-83	
175	Hector Soto	Okuiri	10-14-83	
176	Carl Mangione	Mokuroku	04-25-86	
177	William T. Budde	Okuiri	10-14-83	Northwestern University
178	Elizabeth Cortes	1st Dan	10-14-83	Tae Kwon Do
179	George Benafis	1st Dan	10-14-83	Tae Kwon Do
180	Eileen Adams de Pereira	Kaiden	10-30-93	
181	Ernesto Dennis Richards	1st Dan	12-3-83	Tae Kwon Do
182	Luke Anthony Fabucci	1st Dan	04-27-84	Tae Kwon Do
183	Cesar Mejia Pellerano	Mokuroku	07-8-89	Santo Domingo, D.R.
184	Flavio Vega	Okuiri	01-26-84	Santo Domingo, D.R.
185	Paul M. Ayoub	Okuiri	04-27-84	Northwestern University
186	David G. Feisthammel	Okuiri	04-27-84	Northwestern University
187	Donald P. Koz	Mokuroku	04-10-87	Combat Arts Institute
188	John P. Martin	Mokuroku	04-10-87	Combat Arts Institute
189	D'Arcy Rahming	Kaiden	10-30-93	DePaul University
190	Donald Stone Sade	Okuiri	04-27-84	Northwestern University
191	Jose Negron	Okuiri	04-27-84	
192	Deborah Ann Estrella	Okuiri	10-19-84	
193	Joey Osorio Jr.	Moku Roku	04-24-93	3rd Dan Taekwondo
194	Rafael A. Perez	Okuiri	04-26-85	
195	Joanne Van Cor	Okuiri	04-26-85	
196	Tilo E. Rivas	Okuiri	04-26-85	
197	John E. Sharpe	Okuiri	04-26-85	
198	Luis Antonio Sanchez	Mokuroku	07-16-88	Santo Domingo, D.R.
199	Julio Cordero Lopez	Mokuroku	07-16-88	Santo Domingo, D.R.
200	Otis Waterman Jr.	Okuiri	11-8-85	
201	Robert Galindez Sr.	Okuiri	11-8-85	
202	Jesus B. Lopez	Okuiri	11-8-85	
203	Francisco Javier Rosado	Okuiri	11-8-85	
204	Henry Ortiz	Okuiri	04-25-86	
205	Steve Snelson	Okuiri	04-25-86	Northwestern University
206	David A. Stahlman	Okuiri	04-25-86	Northwestern University
207	Craig A. Kakuda	Okuiri	04-25-86	Northwestern University
208	Louis Bruno	Okuiri	04-25-86	Northwestern University
209	Arthur J. Steinberger	Mokuroku	10-24-92	DePaul University
210	Larry James	Okuiri	04-25-86	Northwestern University
211	C. Allen Reed	Okuiri	04-25-86	Northwestern University
212	Cornelio Bouma Bogaert	Okuiri	07-8-89	Santo Domingo, D.R.
213	Marcos Antonio Nunez	Okuiri	07-26-86	Santo Domingo, D.R.
214	Daniel Arturo Espinal	Okuiri	07-26-86	Santo Domingo, D.R.
215	Adalberto Noble Aquino	Okuiri	07-26-86	Santo Domingo, D.R.
216	Judith T. Serrano	Mokuroku	10-27-90	
217	David L. Taylor	Okuiri	10-24-86	

Advanced Combat Ju-jutsu Pg 225

Black Belt Register

BB#	Name	Rank	Rank Date	Comments
218	Jose Martinez	Okuiri	10-24-86	
219	Barbara Pearson	Okuiri	10-24-86	
220	Mark E. Griffith	Mokuroku	11-11-89	
221	Dennis J. Campo	1st Dan	10-24-86	Tae Kwon Do
222	Ricardo Thomas	2nd Dan	10-27-90	Tae Kwon Do
223	Samuel Hernandez	Mokuroku	04-28-90	
224	Gabriel Cepeda	Okuiri	04-24-87	
225	Guillermo Marranzini	Okuiri	08-03-87	Santo Domingo, D.R.
226	Francisco Rodriguez	Okuiri	06-25-87	Santo Domingo, D.R.
227	Samuel Bisono E.	Okuiri	06-25-87	Santo Domingo, D.R.
228	Louis Medina Rodriguez	Okuiri	10-23-87	
229	John Goodson	Okuiri	10-23-87	
230	Nick Anzelino	Okuiri	10-23-87	
231	Tom Testa	Okuiri	10-23-87	
232	Robert Aviles Jr.	1st Dan	10-23-87	Tae Kwon Do
233	Carlos Munoz	1st Dan	10-23-87	Tae Kwon Do
234	Kevin Campo	1st Dan	10-23-87	Tae Kwon Do
235	Charles Ross	Okuiri	4-15-88	Deceased, 4/89
236	P. David Lax	Mokuroku	10-27-90	
237	Ivan Beras	Okuiri	7-16-88	Santo Domingo, D.R.
238	Carlos Garcia	Okuiri	7-16-88	Santo Domingo, D.R.
239	Soraya Holguin	Okuiri	7-16-88	Santo Domingo, D.R.
240	Pedro Perez	Okuiri	7-16-88	Santo Domingo, D.R.
241	Alejandro Serralle	Okuiri	7-16-88	Santo Domingo, D.R.
242	Luis Taveras	Okuiri	7-16-88	Santo Domingo, D.R.
243	Wesley Colon	1st Dan	10/88	Tae Kwon Do
244	Stanley Wasserman	Okuiri	04-06-89	Honorary
245	Jimmy Perez	Okuiri	06-03-89	
246	Johnny Ayala	Okuiri	06-03-89	
247	Migdalia Laboy	Okuiri	06-03-89	
248	Francisco Laboy	1st Dan	06-03-89	Tae Kwon Do
249	James J. Babowice	Okuiri	5-27-89	Northwestern University
250	David Andrews Mabon	Okuiri	05-27-89	Northwestern University
251	John Chris Angelo III	Okuiri	05-27-89	Northwestern University
252	Alex Liff	Okuiri	05-27-89	Northwestern University
253	Diane Lynn Wallander	Moku Roku	10-30-93	DePaul University
254	Eduardo Diaz	Okuiri	07-08-89	Santo Domingo, D.R.
255	Felix Sabala	Okuiri	07-08-89	Santo Domingo, D.R.
256	Israel Velazquez	Okuiri	07-08-89	Santo Domingo, D.R.
257	Domingo Genao	Okuiri	04-28-90	
258	Gil Avila	Okuiri	04-28-90	
259	Victor A. Lachapelle	Okuiri	04-03-90	Santo Domingo, D.R.
260	Elvin Santiago	Moku Roku	10-30-93	
261	Reginaldo Brown	Okuiri	10-27-90	

Black Belt Register

BB#	Name	Rank	Rank Date	Comments
262	Jose Garcia	Moku Roku	04-24-93	
263	George Lulaj	1st Dan	10-27-90	Tae Kwon Do
264	Candida Aviles	1st Dan	10-27-90	Tae Kwon Do
265	Fernando Reyes	1st Dan	10-27-90	Tae Kwon Do
266	William Keeling	Okuiri	6-22-90	
267	Annibal Reyes	Okuiri	7-24-91	Santo Domingo, D.R.
268	Eric Hasbun	Okuiri	7-24-91	Santo Domingo, D.R.
269	Omar Echevarria	Okuiri	7-24-91	Santo Domingo, D.R.
270	Alex Fernandez	Okuiri	7-24-91	Santo Domingo, D.R.
271	Charles S Whitman	Okuiri	10-26-91	Northwestern University
272	John McIntyre	Okuiri	4-25-92	
273	Joel Valdez	Okuiri	4-25-92	Santo Domingo, D.R.
274	Antonio Gonzalez	Okuiri	4-25-92	Santo Domingo, D.R.
275	Emanuel Perez	Okuiri	10-24-92	
276	Rommel Santana	Okuiri	05/92	Santo Domingo, D.R
277	William Correa	Okuiri	10-30-93	
278	Leonel Contreras	Okuiri	4-24-93	
279	Daniel Hook Jr	Okuiri	4-24-93	
280	Mike Lopez	Okuiri	10-30-93	
281	Nick Harrison	Okuiri	10-30-93	
282	Gamal Newry	Okuiri	10-30-93	

Index

A
About the Author	Pg 10
Aiding someone	Pg 182
Armbars	Pg 50
Atemi Waza	Pg 28 - 30

B
Black Belt Exams	Pg 216 - 219
Black Belt Register	Pg 220 - 226

C
Chokes	Pg 154 - 156
Classical Ju-jutsu	Pg 13
Club defenses	Pg 169 - 174
Compound Kote-gaeshi	Pg 39
Controls	Pg 44

F
Formal throws	Pg 52 - 82
Front body grabs	Pg 133 - 136
Fudoshin:	Pg 18

G
Gokyo	Pg 215
Ground defenses	Pg 190 - 192
Gun defenses	Pg 175 - 179

H
Hand strikes	Pg 28,29
History	Pg 14

I
Introduction	Pg 11
Interview	Pg 15, 16

K
Kansetsu Waza	Pg 45 - 51
Kick defenses	Pg 183 - 185
Kicks	Pg 30
Kihon	Pg 19,20
Knife defenses	Pg 157 - 168
Kote-waza	Pg 31 - 43
Kyu Exams	Pg 205 - 213

L
Lapel grabs	Pg 126 - 130

M
Mugs 1-17	Pg 137 - 153
Multiple man attacks	Pg 180

O
Osae-komi Waza	Pg 83 - 85

R
Rear body grabs	Pg 131,132
Reversals	Pg 197 - 203

S
Sitting defenses	Pg 186 - 189

T
Tai sabaki	Pg 88 - 119
Taiso	Pg 21

U
Ukemi	Pg 22 - 26

W
Wall techniques	Pg 195,196
The Warrior's Strategy	Pg 120, 121
Wrist grabs	Pg 122 - 125

Z
Zanshin:	Pg 17

Order the Complete Miyama Ryu Library

Bookmasters Distribution Services, Dept ACJ
1444 State Route 42 R.D. # 11, Mansfield, Ohio 44903
800-247-6553 or 419-281-1802 • Fax 419-281-6883

Combat Ju-jutsu - The Lost Art
by D'Arcy Rahming

Disable an attacker with striking, kicking, throwing and joint breaking technique. Defend from multiple attackers armed with knives and clubs. Thwart rear mugging attacks. Escape unharmed from wrist, lapel and body grabs. Use body positioning to avoid an attack and then counter-attack. Develop the right attitude for surviving a violent street encounter.

Book (160 pages): $18.95   Video (VHS) 55 minutes $49.95
ISBN: 0-9627898-0-1

The College Student's Complete Guide to Self-Protection
by D'Arcy Rahming

Develop techniques to identify and diffuse potential threats. Increase awareness of your surroundings. Develop your street smarts. Defend yourself with practical yet simple techniques. Ask the right questions about the physical security of on- and off-campus housing.

Book (160 pages): $14.95
ISBN: 0-9627898-2-8

Necessary and Reasonable Force - The Essential Guide for Law Enforcement Officers
by Edward F. Sullivan

Learn which self-defense techniques work best for peace officers and how much force should you use to defend yourself and others. Officer Edward F. Sullivan, a 20 year police veteran and black belt defensive tactics instructor, describes the physical and mental preparation you will need if you are considering a career in law enforcement.

Book (160 pages): $19.95
ISBN: 0-9627898-8-7